Earn Your Influence

Become the Person People Trust, Follow, and Grow With

LINNITA HOSTEN

EARN YOUR INFLUENCE
Become the Person People Trust, Follow, and Grow With

Hardcover ISBN: 979-8-9950315-2-9
Published by Excellence Brainery

Book design, layout, and production by Typepub (www.typepub.com).

DEDICATION

I'm typing this section of the book on a flight headed home from attending a homegoing service of Maurice Antonio Kinsey. A friend I met in 2012 who changed the trajectory of my life. I met Maurice at a work event in 2012. I had just finished a 5th grade middle school assembly and was headed home. Maurice waited until I packed up my materials to approach me to say hello. Well, actually he didn't say hello, he said, "Man, you're gifted! I'm Maurice," as he extended his hand for a handshake. I smiled and thanked him. He followed up and asked, "Have you ever thought about speaking as a business? Like outside of your job?" I laughed and asked, "Who me?"

I heard him clearly, but at that time, I didn't see myself as anything other than an employee who talks to middle and high school students as a part of her job. He asked me if I would be open to meeting up over lunch to talk about building out a speaking career. In my head, this guy was nuts!

I didn't take him seriously. I thought he was just shooting his shot creatively. Well, I accepted his lunch invitation. We met in the atrium of the Gaylord in National Harbor, Maryland. I walked in to meet him, seated at a table with a notebook. This man had a whole plan of how we could do a co-ed student leadership tour. Honestly, I was overwhelmed and felt like his vision was way ahead of my time. And it was.

We ate first, and then we, I mean, HE talked through the plan. I didn't have much to contribute because I was still in disbelief that he was proposing this to me.

I even remembered saying, "I'm too young. People won't even take me seriously." He had an affirming response for all of my insecure objections, which were really wrapped in fear and thoughts of inadequacy. Somehow, Maurice eventually convinced me to believe in myself.

Between 2012-2014, Maurice and I taught *The ABC's of Leadership* to student leaders across the District of Columbia, Maryland, and Virginia until I ran into a period of depression. A few bad decisions in my love life, and with my money started painfully adding up. It caused me to have to move back home with my parents after establishing myself independently. Moving back into a 300-square-foot room was hard. But what was even harder was admitting that I needed the help. I prolonged the decision to move back home for almost a month. Barely wanting to leave bed. I took several days off from work, and even when I returned to work, I could barely focus on my tasks. My manager was even concerned.

During that time, Maurice might have called me every day. I was so annoyed by his persistence. He would challenge me to set one goal to do that day. He did this until I had enough willpower to return to myself. I remember telling him before I came out of my funk, "I don't have it in me to do this anymore. Just let this whole idea go."

Relentlessly, he wouldn't let me.

Fast forward over 13 years later, I'm so glad I didn't allow the embarrassment of my personal failures deter me from pursuing my goals. A few of my goals when I met Maurice were to speak on a college campus, to do a TEDx talk, to write a book, to keynote large conferences, to be known for my work. All of those goals have been met.

I thank God for sending Maurice at a time before I knew who I was capable of even becoming. His belief in me made it very hard for me not to believe in myself.

One of his favorite sayings were, "Always leave someone better than you found them."

Thank you, Maurice, for your belief and generosity. While I could never repay you for your time and money you willingly invested in me, I can make the lives of others better than they were before I encountered them. My prayer is that this book does that for you, reading this. Rest well, my friend.

ACKNOWLEDGMENT

Thank you, Heavenly Father. For your infinite wisdom, guidance, and generosity. Thank you for the talents and gifts you've given me to impact the world for your glory. I pray that my life would lead others to want to get to know you, live for you honorably, and serve you.

Let this book be a tool you use to help others live like your son, Jesus.

TABLE OF CONTENTS

ABOUT THE AUTHOR

Linnita Hosten is a holistic communications coach who equips high-visibility emerging leaders to build trust and grow teams through Earned Influence. With more than a decade of experience across government, corporate, and academic sectors, she has trained over 10,000 professionals, including leaders within the United States Army, National Institutes of Health, the National Society of Black Engineers, and more than 50 colleges and professional associations nationwide.

The 5x author is the founder of Vocal Value, a boutique training and development firm that delivers coaching, workshops, and digital learning programs to help emerging leaders grow their communication competence, clarity, and confidence.

Linnita's signature approach integrates wellness, neuroscience, and storytelling. Grounded in her experience as a Certified Holistic Coach and former college professor who taught communication and public speaking, her work has been featured by TEDx, the National Press Club, and New York Weekly.

She has received more than a dozen honors and awards, including Speaker of the Year, 40 Under 40 in Education, and Alumni of the Year from the University of Maryland Global Campus.

Linnita holds a Bachelor of Science in Mass Communication from Towson University and a Master of Science in Nonprofit Management from the University of Maryland Global Campus.

She is a member of Zion Church in Greenbelt, Maryland, led by Senior Pastor Keith Battle, where she actively serves as a licensed Minister.

A true believer of God's promises, Linnita holds dear to her heart Jude 1:24 *"Now unto him that is able to keep you from falling, and to present you faultless before the presence of his glory with exceeding joy."*

When not speaking, training, ministering, or coaching, you can find the pescetarian in the produce section at your local farmer's market, diving into a good audiobook, browsing online for things she will probably not buy, or enjoying the company of her good girlfriends.

You can connect with Linnita online at LinnitaHosten.com or across social media platforms using the handle @LinnitaHosten.

FOREWORD

"Dang! I wish I had thought of this."

Those were my internal thoughts while reading *Earn Your Influence*. In my line of work, I've read countless books on leadership and influence. Yet as I turned these pages, I found myself not only relating to the stories but seeing my own journey unfold within them.

Before my current career as a professional speaker, I taught in the classroom. At the end of every day, reflection was the discipline that sharpened my craft. I had to sit with every decision, every action, and every word I used. I would ask myself, 'What went well?' What did not go as planned? What can I improve tomorrow?'

Beneath those questions, what I was really asking was: What kind of influence did I achieve?

When Linnita writes, "You can inherit authority, but you cannot inherit influence," she names something leaders often feel but struggle to articulate. Influence is the silent atmosphere that enters and leaves a room with the person who carries it.

The framework Linnita presents is both practical and deeply reflective. While the principles are timeless, they feel especially urgent in a world filled with uncertainty and noise.

If I had access to this book earlier in my journey, I would have treated it as a field guide. Not just something to read, but something to apply daily.

Linnita, your voice is strong and needed. This generation—and the ones to come—will use this book to become not people of power, but people who care deeply for people.

PREFACE

Whether you lead at work, in your church, in a community organization, or within your own family, leadership often begins long before we feel ready for it. Some of us step into responsibility because we were asked. Others step in because we felt a desire to contribute to something bigger than ourselves. Either way, leadership has a way of exposing parts of us we didn't know needed attention.

For a long time, I believed leadership was about being firm, decisive, and strong enough to carry the weight on my own. I've lost opportunities, relationships, and trust by leading from a position rather than a connection. I've also been on the receiving end of leadership that relied more on authority than influence. My experiences have taught me that people comply with authority and grow under its influence.

This book is about earning that influence.

Over the next few pages, I'm inviting you to reflect on who you are when you speak and how your life experiences have shaped the way you communicate. You'll also explore the difference between authority that's given and influence that's earned.

Consider this book a space to slow down and study what's beneath your voice.

I pray that as you read, you gain language for experiences you've felt but never named. And that you grow into a way of leading that allows others to trust you, follow you, and grow alongside you.

SECTION 1: THE HEART OF YOU

"So let's not get tired of doing what is good. At just the right time we will reap a harvest of blessing if we don't give up." (Galatians 6:9, NLT)

CHAPTER 1

FOUNDATIONS OF INFLUENCE

Let's start from the top. I feel like you may know this already, but just in case you may not know, I'm going to share it: You can inherit authority, but you cannot inherit influence. Influence is not something people hand you because you carry a title or because your name sits at the top of an organizational chart. Influence is earned. It is entwined, through the way you speak to people, the way you respond to challenges and changes, and the way you carry yourself when no one is applauding. For years, I believed influence started the day you became "the leader," and people finally saw you in your role. But real influence begins long before the opportunity ever arrives. It starts behind the scenes, in the unnoticed work, in the rooms where no one is evaluating you. It is that unseen preparation that shapes the kind of leader you will eventually become publicly.

If you were to trace the story of any respected leader, you would find the same pattern: a season of obscurity, strength building, and faithfulness—all occurring when it felt like no progress was happening at all. That season (the season most people overlook) is the foundation of earned influence. And if you're reading this book, chances are you're in one of those seasons right now. Maybe you're leading a team at work, organizing volunteers at your church, mentoring students, or juggling the expectations of a community committee. Or maybe you're the person everyone depends on, even though your title doesn't reflect the weight you carry. No matter what your leadership looks like today, I want you to know something important: Your influence is being shaped long before anyone recognizes it. Everything you've lived, served, survived, and learned has contributed to the leader you are becoming.

This truth is seen clearly in the story of David in the Bible. When most people hear his name, they picture Goliath on the battlefield, the giant, the victory. But David's influence didn't begin with the slingshot moment. His foundation was built in the quiet, unnoticed work that nobody valued. David was the youngest of eight brothers, overlooked by his own family and assigned the least glamorous responsibility: tending sheep. He wasn't trained as a warrior, he wasn't old enough to fight, and he certainly wasn't positioned for leadership. Yet it was in those fields away from applause, titles, and the spotlight that David learned to lead, protect, listen, and fight for what mattered. And he learned to trust what he had been given.

While his brothers were positioned on the front lines of battle, David was positioned in an outdoor classroom of preparation. So when he finally stood before Saul and later before Goliath, David didn't draw confidence from theory or talent. He drew confidence from his track record with God. And when Saul questioned David, saying, "…There's no way you can fight this Philistine and possibly win! You're only a boy, and he's a man of war since his youth," (1 Samuel 17:33, NLT). David responded to Saul with evidence, saying: "The Lord who rescued me from the claws of the lion and the bear will rescue me from this Philistine!" What David was conveying to Saul was that he had earned his influence, which came from his unseen experience tending to sheep.

When it was time to go face the Philistine (who was over nine feet tall, Saul tried to dress David in Saul's own armor, suggesting that David's leadership had to look a certain way. David refused and proceeded to the battle with five stones, a staff, and a sling. I believe David's belief that he could defeat the giant outweighed the power of any tool he could use in the fight.

Your influence starting point kicks off the day you take responsibility for the assignment in front of you, no matter how small it seems. The earning of influence is happening when no one is clapping, you're carrying expectations that feel heavy and at times unfair, you're making decisions that cause conflict and require courage, and you're modeling resilience in seasons of uncertainty. People follow leaders whose actions they trust behind their words. They watch how you handle pressure, how you treat others, how you respond to conflict, and how you grow. The more they watch, the more they decide whether or not to follow you.

Influence is demonstrated.

My first introduction to leadership began at sixteen years old in the television studio of my high school. I was appointed News Director for our high school's morning show, a role that required technical skills, quick decision-making, and constant communication. At sixteen, I believed leadership meant dominance and control, and I led from that mindset. I raised my voice when I was frustrated. I called people out publicly. At the time, I believed being firm and aggressive was how leaders earned respect. What I hadn't yet developed was emotional regulation, compassion, or the awareness that true influence is rooted in trust, not fear. Looking back, I realize the teenage version of me was doing her best with the tools she had. And many emerging leaders start in that exact place, trying to prove to themselves they are capable of leading, while unknowingly pushing people away. If that is where you find yourself today, this book is not here to shame you. It is here to help you see where your opportunities for growth truly lie.

After more than fifteen years leading in government, bi-vocational ministry, secondary education, higher education, interscholastic athletics, and hybrid-entrepreneurship, the greatest lesson I have learned is simple: **the most powerful form of leadership is rooted in how you speak to people, not the authority you hold over them.** People follow connection. They follow leaders who help them feel seen, heard, and genuinely valued. They follow the leader who remembers their humanity. That is the heart of earned influence.

This book will teach you exactly how to cultivate that kind of leadership. As you continue reading, you will learn to communicate with confidence and connection so people follow you voluntarily because they believe in you and feel honored to grow with you.

Leadership is an opportunity to do good. Influence is an opportunity to lift others. And your voice, your unique God-shaped voice, is one of the most powerful tools you have been given to do both.

"Therefore, whenever we have the opportunity, we should do good to everyone - especially to those in the family of faith." (Galatians 6:10, NLT)

CHAPTER 2

THE WORK THAT SHAPES YOU

My heart is for the emerging leader. Someone who like David, may currently be doing "insignificant" work. The person who is not the first choice. You may not even be the loudest person or the most creative, but you're capable of leadership. You are full of possibility and undeniable passion- it just might not be your time to be "front-facing" or to run that project or team.

And guess what, that's good news because that means you have the "runway" to grow into the person who is ready for that next opportunity. You might be in a role now that you feel you are overdeveloped for or even running a project that you can do with your eyes closed. The work isn't very challenging, and you hunger for more.

That's a great place to be too. So, while you're waiting, let's build your competency and your capacity.

Building Competency and Capacity

This is what Amanda Brown did for me. Amanda was my first boss, and she embodied the heart of a leader. I was 17 when I met Amanda. She was the store manager at a coffee shop. She came into the store eager to turn our sales numbers around. (I'm guessing she was incentivized through sales commission.) The first thing Amanda did to earn the ability to influence me, she intentionally learned my name and my story. She asked me what my goals were and what I wanted to do while there. The next thing she did was empowered me. I was a 17-year cashier who probably wasn't going to be there too much longer (because my plans were to go to college.) Yet, she still challenged me to become a master at the drink recipes.

She would quiz me on the ingredients for lattes, macchiatos, and different mixed drinks. She would time me doing the recipes. I got so good at the job that I actually loved going there. I grew a hunger for efficiency and customer service.

Amanda taught me to prepare drink orders as customers requested them and, when a line formed, to take orders while customers were waiting and bring them to the cashier. We were so efficient as a team that the line would be wrapped around the store, and our frequent customers were happy to wait because they knew the holdup was only because there were two cashiers (and not because we were moving slow). Most of the time, customers were handed their drinks while they were paying and did not have to wait afterward. As customers grew in trust, so did our tip jars. We had a clear plastic square jar that sat on the counter near the register. Out of appreciation, customers would tip 20, 50, and even 100-dollar bills. I'm not sure if they were generous because our drinks were good or if they were generous because, as a team, we were "good people."

We knew the drink orders of our regulars and their children, and we knew their names. And if you're wondering, we did become the #1 store in the district. Amanda was soooo good that she got assigned to another store, and she eventually later worked her way up to corporate management (so I later learned.)

I wonder if Amanda ever felt insignificant and said things like, "I'm just a coffee store manager. I won't be like this my whole life. This work isn't meaningful. It's just a job." I wonder if she would have experienced greater levels of management or leadership if she had not had the mindset she had.

I wonder whether David would have had the bold audacity to fight Goliath if he had been running from those bears and lions (instead of fighting them). I wonder if David felt, "This is stupid. I'm capable of doing so much more."

It's easy to see our everyday life as *small* and insignificant. But just be reminded that your small piece is big preparation for wherever you may be afforded to go next.

Reminders from God:

- "Work willingly at whatever you do, as though you were working for the Lord rather than for people." (Colossians 3:23, NLT)

- "If you are faithful in little things, you will be faithful in large ones. But if you are dishonest in little things, you won't be honest with greater responsibilities." (Luke 16:10, NLT)

- "Seek the Kingdom of God above all else, and live righteously, and he will give you everything you need." (Matthew 6:33, NLT)

Small Things You Can Do Now

1. Start journaling how you feel while completing your tasks daily. Take note of the tasks that you loathe and the tasks that you enjoy.

2. For the tasks that you enjoy, identify what you like about those tasks.

3. Look for more ways to grow the skills related to the tasks you enjoy. Is there a class you can take or a project you can lead related to that task?

4. Take the initiative to propose ideas that you can execute around your interests.

5. Continue to repeat this to build your competency in the area you enjoy, and over time, your confidence will grow, too.

"...Be strong and courageous. Do not be afraid; do not be discouraged, for the Lord your God will be with you wherever you go." (Joshua 1:9, NIV)

CHAPTER 3

FINDING A VOICE YOU TRUST

When my parents sent me off to college, I'm sure they drove off thinking, "That girl better make this money that we're spending count for something." OK, maybe they didn't say it like that, but I'm almost certain they were thinking it. Simply put, they were anticipating a return on their investment. Not just for the cost of college, but for all the teaching they instilled in me. Like most parents, they hoped that something I would learn on my college campus would soon apply to the "real world," making me employable and helping me gain financial independence. I can still remember my dad saying things like: "You're going to be our next doctor." He was very sure of that, so I'm sure he was a bit concerned when I showed no interest in pharmacy, nursing, engineering, or any field that typically signaled a "secure quality of life."

When I walked onto my college campus, I had already made peace with the fact that I wasn't chasing the typical 'secure' career path. I wasn't interested in high-paying degrees just for the paycheck. I wanted to study something that I actually enjoyed learning about. Something that fascinated me and stimulated my thinking. I chose communication. My dream was to be a journalist, specifically a news anchor. It was special to watch someone speak so eloquently and confidently, even under pressure. As a high school student, I interned at a local television station, and the excitement of the fast-paced, story-chasing newsroom felt like a challenging adventure.

But my dream of becoming a journalist started to blur the moment I sat through my first college journalism class. As I listened to my classmates speak, I noticed something that made me question everything I thought I was capable of achieving. Their voices carried a kind of polish that felt miles away from where I was. Their words flowed effortlessly, their posture was poised, and their presence was commanding. Meanwhile, I was overthinking every sentence, unsure of how to stand and how to sound. I didn't speak like them. I didn't have the verbal confidence they had. And in that moment, I wondered if I even had what it took. It became apparent that there was a large skills gap between who I wanted to be and who I actually was.

There was a voice in my head that said, "This isn't the career for you. You just don't have 'that'." The charisma, the diction, and the ability to capture someone's attention when you speak. But I continued my studies anyway. Instead of changing my major, I kept it, but I shifted my concentration from journalism to marketing.

The next semester, I found myself enrolled in a class that sounded more intimidating than organic chemistry, Public Speaking 101. I didn't even know speaking was something you could be taught. I genuinely thought some people were just born with the magic mic gene and the rest of us were meant to nervously fumble through group presentations forever.

My public speaking class had about 20 students enrolled. On the first day, I glanced at the syllabus: we were scheduled to give 8 speeches within 15 weeks. That actually excited me. I had done plenty of group projects before, but no one ever paid attention to how I actually spoke or carried myself. It was all about the content, not the delivery. No one ever asked, "Did she engage the room?" or "How well did she structure the information presented?"

The idea of getting feedback to improve how I spoke and presented myself was something I was super eager to get. Preparing speeches for that class were my favorite assignments that semester. I would go to the library and creatively think of how to hook my audience from the beginning, how to creatively introduce a prop. I was fascinated with crafting something to share, something that would teach someone something new.

The assignments were progressively challenging. We started with a five-minute introductory speech about ourselves, then moved on to informative speeches about someone else. Next up was the most memorable assignment, the instructional speech. We had 10 minutes to teach our classmates how to complete a task from start to finish.

I decided to teach them something I loved doing at the time, pedicures. When I was younger, my aunt and I would sit in her room and paint our nails. She taught me how to do a French manicure, cut cuticles, dry nails faster, and shape them with a file. To put a twist on my speech, instead of talking to the ladies in the room, I decided to address the men. I remember opening with, "Are there any guys in the room who know what it feels like to have the hard bottom of your lady's foot rub against yours?" I raised my hand to motion for them to mirror the movement if they could relate. About half the room raised their hands and erupted in laughter.

I hooked them. I don't remember everything else I said in that speech, but I remember how I felt when my classmates rose to their feet to give me a standing ovation. I felt proud and excited, and couldn't wait for the next assignment. I realized I was actually good at this.

Later that semester, I saw a flyer for a beauty pageant. The winner would receive a $5,000 scholarship. I knew I could use the help with tuition, so I nervously, but excitedly, applied, not knowing what I was walking into. For three months, I was coached on presence, posture, and speech. I practiced walking in heels with confidence, making eye contact with judges, proper chair seating, and hand gestures. I had to prepare a talent and purchase a formal gown, appropriate swimwear, a business suit, and skin-tone hosiery. I used my financial aid rebate check to buy my pageant materials. Yes, I basically took out a loan to do a pageant, a terrible idea, I know.

Three weeks before the pageant, I called my parents to invite them. It would be the first time I would speak publicly in front of 100+ people, and people I knew. On the day of the pageant, my stomach flipped, my mouth was dry, and I barely slept the night before. Anxious didn't even begin to describe how I felt. If I could have run from that event like Forrest Gump, I would've. I wasn't afraid of being in the pageant, I was nervous about being watched, critiqued, and judged. Whew, I'm getting nervous just telling you about it.

"Why did you sign up for this?" I asked myself as my heart raced, watching families fill the room. Then I saw my family walk in, my mom, dad, my boyfriend at the time, who surprised me by flying in from his college in Ohio, my best friend Jamel, and a few classmates and teammates from my step team.

When it was my time to speak, I stepped up to the mic in my four- inch heels, barely feeling my legs under me. They were trembling so bad, I expected them to give out on stage. My voice was shaky, but I kept going. I scanned the room like every set of eyes mattered, like I needed every person in those 200+ seats to feel what I had to say. And somehow, in the middle of all that fear, I found my rhythm. It didn't feel perfect. But it did feel *powerful.* I walked off that stage not just with the sash, *Miss Congeniality,* Crowd Favorite, but with a new level of belief in myself. I had done the thing I was terrified to do, and that made me feel like I could do anything.

Here's what my college experience taught me about using my voice: Deciding to sit in fear without addressing it is degenerative. It wears on your self-worth and chips away at your identity. It robs you of your audacity to evolve into who you're capable of becoming.

The fear of being rejected. Fear of being wrong. Fear of being too much. Fear of being seen, these fears rob us of our evolution.

Silence might protect you, but it will never grow you.

I did not know Christ as a college student, but if I did, I would have held tight to "This is my command - be strong and courageous! Do not be afraid or discouraged. For the Lord your God is with you wherever you go." (Joshua 1:9, NLT)

My biggest lesson in all of this is that **when we're ready to grow, we have to manufacture the urgency to do so.** We do this by choosing to disrupt the patterns and mental barriers that keep us fearful or feeling inferior with the skills we don't have.

Our confidence won't just show up one day out of nowhere, it grows, little by little, every time you choose to speak up, even when it feels uncomfortable. Through small, brave moments of using your voice, even when your hands shake. Especially when your hands shake.

Every time you choose to speak when it'd be easier to stay quiet, you grow. You gain strength. And slowly, your voice stops being something you fear and starts becoming something you trust.

This book is your soft push to **start where you are. The polished version of you will authentically catch up.**

So, if you've ever sat in a meeting, in a classroom, or in a conversation, and thought, "I wish I had said that," just know: it's not too late. Your voice can still emerge.

CHAPTER 3 EXERCISE: Voice Recovery Journal

Give yourself about 15 minutes to write down a moment, big or small, where you felt like you couldn't speak up. Think back to times at home, at work, in school, or in relationships.

Next to each memory, write what you wish you had said in that moment. Not what you actually said, but the real words that you wanted to come out.

Notice the patterns. What common environments and surroundings make you shrink? What does your shrinking look like? Is it maybe the tone of your voice? The choice of your words?

Now, choose one of those situations and say the words you wanted to say out loud, to yourself, in the mirror, or to someone you trust. Start practicing the version of you who doesn't hold back.

REFLECTION QUESTIONS:

1. Can you remember a moment when you held back something important? What did that silence cost you, and what did it protect you from?

2. Where in your life do you feel the need to "don't do too much"? What's the story behind that?

3. How do you think your voice has changed over the years? What parts of it do you miss or want to reclaim?

4. What does a confident, honest version of your voice sound like? What would change if you used it more often?

"Do not conform to the pattern of this world, but be transformed by the renewing of your mind. Then you will be able to test and approve what God's will is, his good, pleasing and perfect will." (Romans 12:2, NIV)

CHAPTER 4

WHEN DECISIONS COMPOUND

I remember coming home from college during my sophomore year and walking into my parents' bedroom. My dad was at work, and my mom was getting dressed for her day. "Hello, mother," I said, drawing out every syllable, using every muscle in my face like I was hosting a national news broadcast.

Now, this wasn't how I normally spoke. Not at all. Before college, I had no idea you could even alter the way you sounded. It had never crossed my mind that the voice I used, the one that just naturally came out of my mouth, was something I could shape, refine, or even expand. It just was. It lived in me without effort, and until that moment, without any intention to change.

Where I was proudly raised, in Prince George's County, Maryland, one of the wealthiest majority-Black counties in the United States, the way we spoke was part of who we were. Most of my peers around me talked like I did, without obsessing over enunciation, blending syllables into a rhythm that felt uniquely ours. In fact, in some cases, we straight-up made up our own language. It was normal. And honestly, it's still a part of who I am today.

But college exposed me to a different world. At school, I was dropped into a cultural melting pot. My classmates came from every nationality, background, and experience you could imagine. I sat next to students who were privileged, students who had fought their way there, and everything in between. And every voice was different.

Some sounded polished and proper, each word deliberate. Some were bold. Some were a little "rough around the edges," educated, layered with culture and confidence. Not a single voice was exactly like another.

It was there, surrounded by so many different sounds, that I realized I had a choice: I could keep speaking exactly how I always had, comfortable, familiar, safe, or I could grow and step into an evolved voice that had been inside of me all along.

When I came home that weekend and greeted my mom with "Hello, mother," she whipped her head around so fast. She chuckled and asked, "Why are you talking like that?" We both laughed. And honestly, I couldn't blame her. It probably sounded ridiculous. But it felt... empowering.

I explained that I was working on improving my speech. That I wanted the ability to connect not just with people who sounded like me, but with everybody. I wanted the confidence to walk into any room, whether it looked like me or didn't, and be understood. Heard. Respected.

She smiled. She got it. And in that moment, I felt like I was catching a glimpse of who I was becoming.

See, at college, I wasn't just taking classes. I was a student leader, attending leadership programs, camps, and conferences. I was constantly being exposed to different communication styles. Watching, learning, absorbing.

And what did I notice? The leaders who inspired me the most, the Black and Brown community leaders who commanded rooms without raising their voices, weren't speaking "white." They were just talking clearly.

Their diction wasn't a betrayal of who they were; it was a tool they used to be heard by more people, to break down barriers rather than build them.

And maybe deep down, a part of me wished I had what seemed so natural to them. Not the polished, performative kind of communication, but the kind that felt authentic and undeniably powerful.

So, when my mom caught me mid-practice, what she was witnessing was more than just a funny-sounding "Hello mother," She was meeting a version of me who had decided to grow.

That One Decision

Learning to slow down and speak with real intention, not to sound fancy, but to be truly understood, became one of the best investments I made in myself. When people describe my voice today as powerful, commanding, or authentic, it's not because I was born that way. It's because I made a choice to grow my voice in that way.

That one small decision, that tiny moment of, "I want to sound better so I can connect better," set off a domino effect in my life. It changed the way I listened. It changed what I consumed. It changed how I showed up.

I started studying great communicators. I listened differently. I paid attention to tone, to flow, to word choice. I read books about communication. I watched interviews, not just for the content, but for how the speakers delivered it. I attended conferences and absorbed everything I could.

It was like a new hunger had awakened in me, and I was finally feeding it.

And if you're anything like me, there's a version of you that longs for the same thing: To be understood. Not just heard but felt. To know that when you walk into a boardroom, a courtroom, a team meeting, a doctor's office, or even just sit across from someone you love, you can trust that when you open your mouth, people will actually get you.

They'll follow your meaning without you having to repeat yourself. They'll hear the confidence in your tone before you even finish the sentence.

The Other Reality of Your Small Decision

There is an ugly truth about growth that nobody told me about. That truth is that when you start choosing better for yourself, speaking better, thinking better, and dreaming bigger, it can feel a little lonely at first.

When you evolve, you will naturally outgrow some of your most comfortable spaces and long-standing friendships. You'll hear and see the gap between where you are and where you're headed through the friendships you have. It will show through your conversations as you share experiences and perspectives. I know this all too well, and I wish I didn't know this at all.

For some, the gap between where they are and where they'd like to go will feel unattainable and insurmountable to pursue. People who think like this say things like, "Well, this is who I am." "I don't think I can…"

For others who are not paralyzed by fear, they will see the gap between where they are and where they'd like to go and eagerly want to close it. It fires them up and gives them something to aspire to.

Both feelings are normal. Both are the result of growing pains, but only one of them will support the goal of who you are becoming. Which one are you? Does your skills gap feel insurmountable to pursue? Are you eager and fired up at the opportunity to close the skills gap?

If thinking about this challenges you, that deserves to be celebrated; and you deserve to give the becoming version of you next steps. What will you do with the feelings that you have?

Remember this, **the goal isn't to be liked by everyone. It's to be liked by yourself when you walk out of a room**. Do you like the version of who you currently are?

CHAPTER 4 EXERCISE: The Quiet Exit Interview

Grab your journal and imagine you're sitting across from the version of you who used to hold back. The one who second-guessed, who softened her voice, who worried if anyone would hear her, or care. Write her a goodbye letter.

Thank her for how she tried to protect you. Acknowledge where she showed up in your life and how she helped you survive when speaking up felt scary.

Then, be honest about why you're ready to move forward. Tell her you're choosing a voice that doesn't shrink or second-guess. A voice that trusts itself to be clear, bold, and heard.

After that, write your next chapter.

In one paragraph, describe how you will show up from now on, in your conversations, your meetings, your moments of discomfort. Next to that, find a scripture that supports that characteristic of Christ. What does He say about the attribute you'd like to display?

And when you're done, read it aloud. Then read it to your good girlfriend. The one who is eager to always support you.

This is your start to affirm who you are becoming.

ADDITIONAL REFLECTION QUESTIONS

1. If I spoke from a place of truth, what new opportunities, relationships, or healing could open up?
2. Who or what is really calling the shots when I hold back my voice?
3. What new spaces might welcome me if I fully owned this voice?
4. Who am I becoming by choosing to speak with intention?

Let's Shift Gears

To step into the kind of impact you're meant to have, the real you has to live in how you lead.

So, before we talk about how you communicate, we have to get honest about who's showing up.

Is it the real you, or the version you felt you had to become?

If you're unsure about which version is showing up, ask yourself this one question:

Does my confidence or belief about myself shift based on the room I'm in?

If the answer is yes, my next question is, why does your confidence change?

I wish I was there with you to hear your response and help you process your raw thoughts. These are the kinds of questions that open the door to deeper understanding; and are common questions I ask my coaching clients - to help them get to the root of their communication/confidence barriers.

Just know that most of us learned how to speak, listen, stay quiet, or take up space long before we ever thought about leadership. Those lessons came from the environments we grew up in and the dynamics we learned to navigate.

In the next chapter, we're going to look at where those communication habits started and how they've followed you into adulthood.

"Yet you, Lord, are our Father. We are the clay, you are the potter; we are all the work of your hand." (Isaiah 64:8, NIV)

CHAPTER 5

OWNING YOUR EVOLUTION

Before we ever learn to introduce ourselves, we're already learning how to communicate. The tone of our parents' voices. The way our teachers, coaches, or mentors corrected our behavior. The way people around us listened, or didn't. We absorb their language and delivery without even realizing it. It becomes engrained into who we are until we're ready to shape it for ourselves.

Think about it, when you were growing up, did you get to choose the language you were surrounded by? Did you get to choose the emotions attached to the language in the form of encouragement or even criticism? Whether the adults in your life were warm or cold?

We do not get to choose the environments that raise us and teach us the skill of communication. We simply adapt to the environments we are a part of.

Some of us grew up in homes where our words were celebrated, conversation was a sport, and speaking up was normal. Some of us grew up in spaces where words were used as weapons, or where silence was survival. And without realizing it, that early blueprint becomes the foundation for how we show up later in life.

Sometimes, the communication style we adopt is not a mirror of what we saw. Sometimes it's the complete opposite. We become overly accommodating, overly agreeable, overly accepting, because it feels safer to be considerate of others than to be disappointed that others may not be or cannot be considerate of us.

"I'll make sure no one ever feels unheard the way I did," is the intent that we have.

But what I've learned through years of therapy and coaching is that when I am overly considerate and accommodating, I expedite the diminishing of my own views, feelings, and voice.

Speak Up or Burst Out

Diminishing my voice starts off with small internal dismissals of my thoughts and feelings. They are sooo subtle and, "not that serious" at first. When in a team environment, over time, I began to train the people I work with to accept the absence of my voice as a norm. Usually, this translates to, "Oh, she won't mind." Or "I know she will do it if I ask." I'd find myself in situations that I did not truly agree with, but out of fear of being uncomfortable sharing my truth, I'd go along.

This really came to light for me in the pandemic.

In 2021, during a fast, I received instructions to start a Scholarship Fund. So, I called a friend of mine who deeply enjoys philanthropy.

I told her, "The Holy Spirit told me to start a scholarship fund. Would you be interested in partnering? We could collect and disperse the funds through your nonprofit."

She was just as excited as I was. We had that conversation in January. In February, we were building out the scholarship criteria, application process, and marketing campaign. In the first year of the scholarship fund, we raised over $3000 from sending emails, text messages, and posting on social media. IT. WAS. HARD.

Continually asking for money and having the public pressure of promising that we were going to give something that we did not yet have. The fear of letting people down or having to retract the scholarship was a kind of pressure that robs you of your sleep and eats away at your thoughts throughout the day.

But, by the grace of God, we were able to give away two scholarships! I'm getting excited again just typing this because that was a measure of success that absolutely took an act of courage.

We were so inspired by the generosity of others that we decided to do it again the following year. Getting a bit more tactical, we committed to contributing $1,500 each to kick-start our funding goal so we could reach the new goal of $5,000. We kept all the criteria the same, but we ramped up our marketing efforts.

The second time around, we had fewer contributors, but those who did give, gave larger amounts. One of my clients contributed $1,000! My partner's biggest client gave $800.

When we met the $5,000 so quickly, my partner suggested that we adjust the goal to $10,000 to give away more scholarships. Not a bad idea, right? Considering that we both wanted to support the education goals of students. However, at the time, I knew I would be going into a travel season for speaking across college campuses. Active campaigning to fundraise would be very hard for me to commit to, but I never spoke up about that.

I went along with the increased fundraising goal. Then, we got to the end of the campaigning season, and our funds were shy of $10,000. My partner at the time said, "We'll just each increase our contribution by an additional $500 to meet the goal." And my skin started boiling.

Immediately, I bursted out, "I'm not doing that," with anger. When the words left my lips, I had an immediate revelation that I never spoke up to share how I felt about the goal post being moved throughout the fundraising campaign.

I went along with the increased fundraising goal even though it deeply bothered me.

It felt like our mutual "do good" work was turning into greed for acknowledgement. In my mind, our initial $5,000 goal was plentiful and fulfilling enough, but to my partner, more could be done. Was I wrong for being content? Was she wrong for being ambitious?

I ended up apologizing to my partner for my brash and short-tempered response to adjusting our contribution amounts.

What I learned from that experience is that **when you feel something, say something.** If you don't agree, say that. Suppose you have another idea, share that. If you feel something could be done better, encourage that. We call this speaking up, keeping it straight up, or being real.

Speaking up is a behavior I had to grow into as an adult - after accepting that two people can bring their thoughts and feelings to the table without someone else's being invalidated.

I can share my feelings, and the person I am communicating with can share theirs. And furthermore, even if there is no safety in the relationship for me to express myself without being judged or dismissed, I am still responsible for owning and responding to the feelings that come up.

Ownership of Your Feelings

Being responsible for owning and responding to the feelings that come up when communicating can look like the following:

- Journaling to explore the root of your feelings.

- Talking out your thoughts to someone who can be objective about the situation

- Pausing to ask yourself, "Why did that bother me the way that it did?"

- Then, if necessary, share what you've processed with the person with whom you encountered the uneasy feeling.

My Girl: A Big Influence

My biological father's family is from the West Indies- specifically a small island called Carriacou, an island of the Grenadine Islands. It is a part of the nation of Grenada. It's a place where everyone knows everyone's family, and families have their own mom and pop businesses. Life happens at a slower pace. Clothes are washed by hand and hung to dry daily. Food is made by slaughtering animals and cooking them outside. The water comes from a well, and it is not heated. Homes are built without HVAC systems, so there is no heating or air conditioning. They are built with openings that allow air to pass through – as well as insects.

That is where my grandmother was raised and where she gave birth to five sons. My grandfather was a policeman for the small parish. My grandmother was home raising the boys. She cooked, cleaned, and did what we would call today as "house management."

Eventually, my grandparents moved to "The States" and settled in Brooklyn, New York, where immigrant families found opportunities to earn money and provide for their families. When I visited my grandmother in NY, she would cook two full meals a day from scratch. She would walk to the market, buy perch fish, fresh broccoli, onion, peppers, carrots, garlic, chicken breast, etc.

She would go home and, that same day, cook up a delicious meal. THEN she would plate a serving dish with cutlery, an iced beverage, and a napkin.

"Go and eat now," she'd say.

Basically, I was getting Ritz Carrolton treatment in an income-based New York high-rise apartment by my grandmother. She did this for all her guests. Even guests brought to her home that she didn't particularly care for. This behavior was normal for her. Back home, in her native country, hospitality and service from women was the norm for those who entered a home.

When I would finish, she would take my plate, wash the dishes, and ask me if I wanted some tea. Then she would clean the kitchen and do it all again, starting with breakfast. In my adult years, when I started hosting friends over, I noticed I would make their plate, give them a folded napkin with a beverage. Then I would make myself tea and ask them if they wanted some tea or a dessert. Because this was my childhood norm, it became my adulthood norm.

Now that is an example of a domestic behavior I unconsciously model. There are plenty of other behaviors that I inherited and modeled from my grandmother, parents, a few great teachers, supervisors, and coaches. Some behaviors I have fought to unlearn, and some communication traits I am very proud to have.

Here are some of the communication traits I inherited and *unlearned*:

1. **Fighting back my true emotions when other people are emotionless.** When I became serious about wanting a committed relationship that led to marriage, I realized that I didn't have a norm of expressing myself without being angry. I only had a 1 and a 100. No language for the in-between.

2. **Feeling like I have to engage in communication before I have processed my initial thoughts.** As I've gotten older, I've become more aware that I need time to develop language that explains my feelings. Rarely am I able to just in-the-moment, give a true *and rational* why for something that I am feeling. Releasing the pressure to respond on-the-spot has been

so freeing. I'm way more in-tune to my thinking process when I have time to digest my thoughts. Which also means I can eventually share my feelings objectively and rationally, even when I'm upset.

Here are two communication traits that I am very proud to have inherited:

1. **I feel comfortable having deep conversations with others– whether it's about myself or about them**. Personal reflection was something that was modeled by my mom. She was never ashamed or too prideful to share when she made a mistake or missed the mark.

2. **I do not fear vulnerability. I speak freely about how I feel (when I do speak up)**. If I don't have the money, I advocate for low-cost outings, or I stay home. If I don't have the energy, I tell the person I'm communicating with, "My capacity is limited today."

Your Personal Inventory

What makes up your voice, and how does that impact how you show up today?

I challenge you to reflect on who raised you, who you admire, even who you've tried to emulate. Then reflect on the core of who you really are. If you're wondering how, here's how you can get started:

Ask Deeper Questions

- Who am I, really?

- What matters to me?

- How do I want to make people feel when I speak?

- What kind of impact do I want to leave behind?

Your communication style lays the foundation for the kind of life, leadership, and legacy you want to build.

It all starts with knowing who you're showing up as, **and why.**

CHAPTER 5 EXERCISE: The Communication Style Blueprint

Take a few minutes to reflect on the environments you grew up in:

- How did the people around you communicate?

- What styles did you admire? What styles did you quietly resent?

- What early communication experiences do you notice showing up in how you communicate today, if any?

- What habits might you need to unlearn to step into your desired communication style?

Now, think about you. Who are you becoming? What kind of communicator do you want to be?

In the space below, write a one-paragraph description of your ideal communication style. Describe it like you're describing a future version of yourself. Make it vivid.

____

____

____

____

POWER REMINDERS

- Your voice reflects who you are, not just where you come from.
- You get to choose how you show up.
- You can evolve beyond what shaped you.

"You are the light of the world. A town built on a hill cannot be hidden. Neither do people light a lamp and put it under a bowl. Instead, they put it on its stand, and it gives light to everyone in the house. In the same way, let your light shine before others, that they may see your good deeds and glorify your Father in heaven." (Matthew 5:14–16, NIV)

SECTION 2: THE ART OF YOU

"Observe people who are good at their work – skilled workers are always in demand and admired; they don't take a backseat to anyone." (Proverbs 22:29, MSG)

CHAPTER 6

YOU CAN'T PERFECT WHO YOU PRETEND TO BE

When I started my career as a professional speaker, I actually never sat down to determine "who" I was going to bring into every room, like my values and perspective. Those were not things I defined in the early stages. So, I guess it's no surprise that somewhere along the way, "me" started getting filtered. I wasn't showing up as my full self. I was showing up as the person I thought people would pay for.

I believed, without ever being told, that if I wanted to book more high paying speaking engagements, connect with more audiences, and grow my brand, I had to mold myself into someone who was universally palatable, which really meant safe.

Here's what I mean. Now, I'm an R&B and gospel music girlie. I grew up with soul in my speakers and percussion in my blood. But when it came time to curate the music for my events, I swapped out what I loved for what I thought would "work." Playlists that were more… neutral and generic. Appealing to the mostly white American audiences I was speaking to through a speaker's agency that worked with colleges across the country.

I even started watching shows I never would've watched on my own. White sitcoms. Stand-up comedy. I was studying white American culture. I wanted to understand their sense of humor, their joke references, and what mattered to them.

And it worked. At least, it looked like it did. I started incorporating phrases I heard on those shows, sprinkling in popular white cultural references into my talks. My feedback surveys received 4- to 5-star reviews, and many clients became repeat clients. One college even brought me back three years in a row. That kind of response would normally feel like a win, and professionally, it was.

But personally? It started to feel exhausting.

The kind of fatigue that comes from pretending to be "ok" versus just saying "I'm not ok." Every time I stepped into those rooms, I had to hype myself up, because internally I didn't have enough belief that the real version of me was good enough.

Instead of perfecting who I was. I was perfecting who I was pretending to be.

Let me be clear, this wasn't a total character flip. I wasn't putting on an accent or becoming someone unrecognizable.

But I was editing parts of me that made me *me* and leaning into the parts that felt more comfortable for the crowd in front of me.

I started using words I wouldn't use in real conversations. I danced into rooms when invited to the stage. I cracked jokes I didn't find funny. I threw out catchphrases and mantras just to feel "relatable." I raised my voice more than necessary to feel like I was commanding the room.

And maybe that's what people mean when they say, "stage presence." But in hindsight, it was an inauthentic presence.

The wildest part? No one ever asked me to do that. When I signed with the agency, they didn't say, "Change who you are." They signed me as I was. That should've been the confirmation that I was enough.

But here's what I've learned: Sometimes **the loudest pressure doesn't come from outside, it comes from within.**

It's the inner voice that whispers: You're good, but you'd be better if you were more like them. If you want to stay booked, you've got to make yourself more palatable for them. Just tweak this one thing, and then you'll be more accepted.

That voice is dangerous. Over time, it creates a runway that pulls you away from your identity, leaving you disconnected from who you are. And for me, I was slowly beginning to see and own that I was made in the image of Christ. That the Holy Spirit resting inside of me would rise up and allow me to "be" in any room.

The Shift in My Thinking

The shift didn't happen all at once. But it started when I became a Certified Holistic Wellness Coach in 2024.

Through that process, I learned why we perform. I learned how adaptation is often a trauma response. How we curate our personalities to avoid rejection. How we try to earn safety through acceptance?

I also learned that security, real, grounded, internal security, frees us from that cycle. When you know you're enough, you don't have to *seek* approval or *behave* for acceptance.

And that program? It changed me, again. It reminded me that **pretending to be aligned is not the same thing as being aligned.**

So, I made another decision. This time, I didn't make it for the bookings. I made it for me.

I stopped perfecting the version of me that wasn't real. I embraced the version of me that was already whole.

I'm Caribbean American. I love Soca, GoGo, Dancehall, Afro Beats, anything with a rhythm that shakes the room before I even walk in. That's what's playing on my event playlists now. I speak in my natural Maryland accent. I don't dance onto stages. I don't force jokes.

I don't raise my voice to be heard. I speak from my core. And the people who are meant for it? They get it.

BE WHO YOU ARE

You cannot perfect who you're pretending to be. You can only grow by showing up consistently in your truth.

When I coach clients on communication, I tell them this: "I'm going to show you the dos and don'ts. But you will decide what you adopt. Because your communication style has to match you."

The same goes for you.

You can admire other communicators. You can be inspired by speakers, leaders, and voices that move you. But if you're not showing up as yourself, a disconnect will always exist between who you are and what you are performing as.

EXERCISE: The Stage Self vs. The Real Self

Take out your journal and draw a line down the center of the page.

On the left side, write "The Version I Perform." On the right, write "The Version That Feels Like Me."

Now, think about how you speak in public, at work, or in professional settings: What do you do or say to "win the room"? What parts of your style feel natural, and what parts feel like they're being performed? What habits have you picked up just to make yourself more "relatable" or acceptable? Record these thoughts and reflections on the left side.

Then reflect on the right side: What's your natural communication style when you're comfortable? What kind of language, humor, tone, or presence actually feels like you? How can you begin bridging the gap between these two versions?

DEEPER REFLECTION QUESTIONS:

1. What parts of your communication style have been shaped by trying to "fit in"?
2. Who do you feel safest being your full self around and why?
3. What would change in your life if you fully trusted your real voice to lead the room?
4. What environments make you feel the need to perform, and which ones let you exhale?

POWERFUL REMINDER

You don't need to perform to be powerful.

"For that reason, I want you to remember the spiritual gift that God gave you when I put my hands on you. Use that gift more and more to serve God well. Be strong, because God has given us his Spirit. And his Spirit does not cause us to be afraid. Instead his Spirit causes us to be powerful to serve God. He helps us to love God and other people. And he helps us control ourselves properly." (2 Timothy 1:6, EASY)

CHAPTER 7

THE COST OF OWNING YOUR FAITH

Usually, your faith and your work are not culturally acceptable to collide. We've been taught to keep them separate, to draw a line between what we believe and how we build our careers, and for years, I did just that, until I didn't want to anymore. As I began maturing in my faith, that meant I also no longer cared to hide the "other parts" of me.

The First Encounter

In my first professional role out of college, my job was similar to that of an organizational spokesperson. I was hired to go out and talk about a new education initiative. My target audience was middle and high school administrators, state legislators, teachers, parents, students, and community leaders who supported middle and high school students. My job was to spread a specific message to this group, to get them to care, to believe in what I was saying, and ultimately to take action. For three years, I was learning, stretching, practicing, and discovering creative ways to reach this group.

When I was not speaking and presenting, I was meeting with potential partners to build relationships and expand the reach of our message. It was during one of those times that I met Raymond Harrod.

He was a program manager at a well-known nonprofit at the time, and we worked closely together. Raymond was also a minister at his church, and he was open about his faith.

One day after a staff meeting, I told Raymond, "I want to talk more openly about my faith, but I never know what to share. What's appropriate and what's not?" He smiled and simply said, "You'll know when and what to share as you grow." That was it. No rules. No checklist. Just the truth in one sentence.

About five years later, I started sharing more of my faith online. I was sharing what I believed and what kept me grounded. And then I got a call from my agency.

"Hey, Linnita. The post you just shared about God, we'll need you to take that down. Our stakeholders will be viewing your content, and we want to make sure what you share doesn't offend them."

I didn't like it, but I took the post down. Back then, I didn't think much of it. But now, looking back, it bothers me. It bothers me because **I used to believe that bending who I was was the price of success.** Those compromising pieces of myself were the trade-off I had to make. That if I wanted more money, recognition, and clients, I had to mute some of the parts of me that gave me identity, peace, joy, and strength.

It's wild how we can abandon the very thing that holds us up for the sake of acceptance. I think about this often when I see celebrities in interviews or at events. I find myself wondering, "What part of their voice did they have to abandon to reach success?"

I was compartmentalizing the very thing that was sustaining me through my poor financial decisions, my insurmountable debt at the time, my season of depression, heartbreak, and burnout. I knew then, and I know now, that it wasn't me holding it all together. It was God's sovereign hand and love that corrected and carried me.

You Will Sacrifice Something

In 2022, I left my home church. And if you're wondering if something happened, the answer is no. Nothing happened. I was simply hungry for deeper and more practical teaching.

The most painful part of this process was hearing my home church leadership ask, "Are you leaving here to grow your business?" Their question didn't feel curious, it felt like an accusation. Like I wasn't transitioning to a new place for the right reasons. They implied I was chasing a "bigger" audience, chasing influence for influence's sake. I was offended by the idea. The truth is, I wasn't leaving for my business. I was leaving for myself. I was leaving for growth.

I started visiting a nondenominational church. The way the message was shared, in a conversational tone, appealed to me. The pastors were teaching, they weren't yelling, they were talking in a voice I could follow from start to finish, and I LOVED that.

Eventually, I joined what some might call a mega church, but it didn't feel mega to me. For the first two years, I served in Youth Ministry. That was my comfort zone. I had supported the Youth Ministry at my home church for nine years, so I could do that with my eyes closed.

Then the Youth Pastor at my new church invited me to join his leadership team. I was skeptical. I knew leadership came with expectations, accountability, and a level of responsibility that I wasn't sure I was ready for. I didn't want the extra weight. I just wanted to attend service, take notes, and go home. I wanted to grow at my own pace, on my own terms. I wasn't looking for a title, and I certainly wasn't looking for more eyes on me. But sometimes, God nudges us into spaces we didn't plan for, and that is exactly what was happening.

But that season didn't last long. My Youth Pastor eventually tapped me on the shoulder again and said, "I think you should check out the upcoming minister's class."

I wish you could feel the triggers that went off in my body. Immediate resistance. Anxiousness. Worry. All the feelings. I didn't say anything to him, but I felt it. I signed up for the class, but I wasn't excited. I was fearful.

The day of the orientation, I remember it was a rainy day. I pulled up to the church and parked. I was about 45 minutes early. I sat in my car and cried heavy tears. I wasn't ready to give up what I wanted: my time, my freedom, my vision for how I thought God wanted to use me. I didn't want the weight of ministry, praying for others, officiating funerals, leading ministries, visiting the sick, and being accountable for my spiritual growth. I just wanted to learn God's word, live for Him, and do my business.

Eventually, I dried my eyes and went inside. About 80 people were in the room, there to learn about the process and decide if it was what God wanted for them.

That day shifted my understanding of what ministry really is. It wasn't just a title. It was a mandate for all believers to "…go and make disciples of all the nations, baptizing them in the name of the Father and the Son and the Holy Spirit. Teach these new disciples to obey all the commands I have given you. And be sure of this: I am with you always, even to the end of the age." (Matthew 28:19-20, NLT). We call this the Great Commission.

For years, I believed that teachers of the Bible were majestically set apart. That God whispered in their ear at the age of 5 during their night's slumber and said, "You will preach the Gospel." I learned that wasn't the full truth, nor was it the only way God spoke to His children and provided direction.

I committed to the 18-month Minister in Training class. I sat among men and women who knew the Bible inside and out. They understood the stories, the terms, and the concepts. I didn't. This was an area of growth for me, but I felt excited to learn.

Eventually, I completed the class and was licensed into ministry in October 2024. My family and friends were there to witness this new chapter. This wasn't the "professional speaker" standing on stage. This was God's child, showing up to tell others about Him.

Today, you can search my name online, and you'll know I'm a Christian. Not because it's in my bio, but because it's in my way of living and my messaging.

I finally feel free to share my faith, not just online, but in my events and my teachings. I share it not because I want you to believe, but because I believe. It's who I am. My whole "self" shows up when I communicate. Yours should, too.

What Owning My Faith Has Taught Me

Even if we have a vision for ourselves, God's purpose will always win. It's not always what we expect. It's not always on our timeline. No matter how inadequate or inexperienced you feel, no matter how much you try to plan your own way, you cannot outrun the assignment of your life. The calling God has placed on you is ingrained, imprinted onto your very existence, and eventually, if willing, you will surrender and grow into the fullness of what you've been designed to do.

"For God's gifts and his call are irrevocable." (Romans 11:29, NIV)

There is no "look" for the work you were born to do. There might be a "look" that others expect, but that's not your concern. You were designed uniquely, and you don't have to do anything extra to get what's already yours.

"For we are God's handiwork, created in Christ Jesus to do good works, which God prepared in advance for us to do." (Ephesians 2:10, NIV)

Maybe you don't have a faith practice. Maybe your challenge is just accepting that you have what it takes to do the thing in you that you enjoy and desire to grow.

If that's you, know this: the "cheat code" for bold self-belief is belief in something bigger than you.

Consider taking a Spiritual Gifts assessment. Ask God to give you clarity and direction regarding how he would like to use you. And trust that what you've been given is enough.

REFLECTION QUESTIONS:

1. Where do you feel most like yourself, and where do you feel the need to edit or protect parts of who you are?
2. How does performing for acceptance affect your energy, confidence, or sense of peace?
3. What small shift could help you communicate more honestly and in alignment with who you truly are?

"In his grace, God has given us different gifts for doing certain things well…" (Romans 12:6, NLT)

CHAPTER 8

WHAT PEOPLE EXPERIENCE WHEN THEY SEE YOU

In 2023, I had an idea to host a public speaking class. The first thought that crossed my mind was, "Girl, who do you think you are? Oh, now you're a teacher all of a sudden?" Whew! That inner critic that lives inside all of us really does not want you or me to win, at all!

Eventually, I faced my fear. I put together a curriculum, built a landing page, and decided to go for it. I priced my tickets at $199 for early bird and $249 for general admission. Seven people signed up. One person even reached out and asked if I had a VIP option, which I didn't.

I remember asking a good friend at the time, "What could I even offer for VIP?" He shrugged and said, "I don't know, but it sounds like she just wants extra time with you." So that's exactly what I gave her.

When I hosted that event, I was genuinely surprised. Half of the room was people I didn't know. One person had even traveled from out of state to be there. I was beta-testing whether people would actually show up, whether they would trust me to teach something I loved, and whether I was even qualified to do this. And I proved to myself that I could.

Fast forward to today: I've worked with over 100 students through my virtual and in-person classes. And it's always the same conversation. No matter where they're from or what their background is, they all tell me some version of the same challenge:

"I want to sound more polished. I want to feel confident when I'm speaking. I want people to take me seriously. I want to avoid the 'umms' and 'ahhs'. I want to command a room. I want to stop being so nervous."

Almost every student can relate to at least four out of six of those statements. And it opened my eyes. So many people are using public speaking every single day, but they're doing it fearfully, anxiously, and without confidence.

That's what I wanted to change.

And if you're reading this, I know you're probably ready for me to finally start breaking down the how. But I need you to trust me on this: spending time understanding your "who" before jumping into the how is going to put you way ahead of where I was when I started.

Let's jump into the art of communication and how you use it to earn your influence.

One of my private coaching students taught me something that completely reframed how I look at communication. He was a trumpet player in a competitive performing band. He told me his band director used to say, "People hear with their eyes," when giving horn section directives about their body movement during performances. His band director was reminding the instrumentalists that how they sound is not the only area of their performance being evaluated. How they look matters too.

When you hear that, it almost feels unfair. But when you really sit with it, you realize how true it is. The moment you stand in front of an audience, whether that's one person or a thousand, they're not just listening to you. They're watching you. They're scanning everything: how you stand, how you move, how you are dressed, how you carry yourself, long before your words begin to leave your lips.

Studies show that people form impressions within milliseconds of seeing someone. Often, they decide whether they trust you based on your appearance, posture, and body language before a single word is spoken. In fact, researchers at Princeton found that it takes just a tenth of a second to make a judgment about someone's trustworthiness (Willis & Todorov, 2006).

People are deciding whether or not they trust you based on what they see before they even decide to process what you're saying. It's not always a fair game, but it's one I want you to be aware of. The sooner you become aware of it, the sooner you can take ownership of what you can control.

This is why I push students who take my classes and workshops; and clients who invest in my coaching programs, I push them to study themselves. To study their bodies. To study how they communicate physically, because your body will tell the truth even when your mouth wants to pretend. Your body reveals your confidence, your anxiety, your fatigue, your excitement, all of it.

When I work with clients, we break their visual competency into four specific areas to master:

Your Feet Tell the First Story.

Most nervous speakers, you'll find them pacing or rocking. They'll walk back and forth excessively. It's a clear sign of discomfort. Your body is trying to release tension through motion.

Are you a pacer? You won't know until you review a recording of yourself. Once you do, here's what to keep in mind: your feet should be planted and facing your audience. The direction of your feet often indicates the direction of your attention. If you tend to fidget or shift, consider wearing stable shoes. Avoid heels that are too high, narrow, or slippery. Ladies, if your feet are sliding forward in your shoes, that discomfort will show up in your body language.

As a feminine woman, I wear heels when I speak, but I try to choose a platform heel or something with a soft arch that keeps me balanced.

Then Come Your Hands

Hand gestures are powerful, but they need intention. Too much movement can be distracting. But intentional hand gestures that align with your words can help drive your message home. If you're unsure how your hands move when you speak, watch a recording and focus solely on that. Do your gestures match the meaning of your words? Are they helping or hurting your delivery?

Posture

Posture tells on you, too. Fatigue shows up in your shoulders first. When you're tired or unsure, your body leans in, slouches, or collapses inward. Try standing in front of a mirror and tell your body to stand tall. Focus on the placement of your back, shoulders, and chin. Feel that positioning. Store it in your body like your favorite driver's seat setting in the car. That's your posture baseline. When you're not in front of a mirror, recall how that felt and reset.

Eye Contact

This one is my favorite to coach on. I can always tell who the speaker feels safest with in the room because that's who they'll look at the most. But eye contact isn't just about comfort, it's about connection. Avoiding eye contact sends a signal to your audience that you're either nervous or not too confident in what you're saying. And if you wouldn't trust someone who couldn't look you in the eye, why should they trust you?

Eye contact is the quickest way to create intimacy. It says, "I see you," and it turns a presentation into a conversation.

One of my favorite tricks is to make eye contact with as many people in the room as possible. It helps to make each person feel like you are speaking directly to them. The effect is powerful and personal.

When you study your body, how you breathe, how you stand, how you gesture, you start gathering insights. Those insights spark awareness. That awareness is data that you can begin to use to establish intentional control. And that ability to have visual control is what builds your confidence over time.

When you know how your nerves show up physically, you can train your body to respond and support your messaging instead of sabotaging it.

This is why I emphasize mastering your who before your how.

People don't follow you because you speak perfectly. They follow you because they trust you. And usually, because you feel real.

Try It for Yourself

Take out your phone. Record yourself speaking. Play it back with no sound. What is your body saying before your words even leave your lips? Are you shrinking? Rushing? Leaning? Then play it again with sound. Pay attention to your energy. Where are you strong? Where are you hesitant?

You can also identify a communicator you admire and observe them closely. How do they use posture, movement, and eye contact? What makes their presence magnetic?

This exercise is about building your personal visual competency so your body and its messaging are in alignment.

Believe it or not, the way your body communicates teaches people how to receive you before you ever say a word.

So, master your visual competency first.

REFLECTION QUESTIONS:

1. Which of these visual skills comes most naturally to you? Which one needs more development?

2. How do your nerves show up physically when you speak?

3. Have you ever watched a recording of yourself presenting? What stood out?

4. When do you feel most confident while speaking?

But Moses pleaded with the Lord, "O Lord, I'm not very good with words. I never have been, and I'm not now, even though you have spoken to me. I get tongue-tied, and my words get tangled." Then the Lord asked Moses, "Who makes a person's mouth? Who decides whether people speak or do not speak, hear or do not hear, see or do not see? Is it not I, the Lord? Now Go! I will be with you as you speak, and I will instruct you in what to say." (Exodus 4:10-12, NLT)

CHAPTER 9

BUILDING TRUST THROUGH YOUR VOICE

Let's talk about vocal competency. This is the area that most people are concerned about. They're worried about how they sound. Do I sound like I know what I'm talking about? Do I sound confident? Will people take me seriously? They want to make sure that the way they put their words together, that it communicates authority, trust, and clarity.

A huge part of vocal competency comes down to articulation and pronunciation. We've all picked up speech patterns from our families, our environments, and our communities. If you grew up around people who mumbled, spoke fast, or didn't emphasize the correct sounds of words, you might find it harder to naturally articulate certain words. And that's okay.

> **Let's Be Clear**
>
> Speaking articulately is not about "sounding white" or mirroring a certain identity. Speaking articulately is about clearly using your words in a way that's true to your dialect and identity. You can honor where you're from and still practice clarity. (As a child of an immigrant parent, I whole heartedly stand by this.)

One of the easiest ways to improve your articulation is to slow down.

Your lips, your tongue, your jaw, and the muscles in your face all work together to shape your words. When you slow down, you give your body a chance to sync up and support your verbal delivery.

Think of your speech as a series of micro movements that function in synchronization.

Tongue Twisters

Want to improve your articulation? Try tongue twisters like "Peter Piper picked a peck of pickled peppers." They challenge the clarity of your speech and help to train your mouth for more precise delivery. Even simple mouth exercises like stretching your jaw and warming up your lips can help you sound more clear and in control.

Eliminating Filler Words

Now let's talk filler words, those pesky "umms," "uhs," and "like." The most common question I get in my class is, "How do I stop saying those?"

My answer: get comfortable with silence.

We often rush to fill quiet moments because we're afraid of sounding unsure. While rushing through our words, in moments where we are thinking of what to add or say, we fill in those gaps with filler phrases or words.

Examples of Filler Phrases:

- You know what I mean
- In my opinion
- To piggyback off of what you said
- If that makes sense
- And stuff like that

Examples of Filler Words:

- Basically
- Like
- So
- Well
- Umm
- Ah
- Er
- Uh

I want to empower you by sharing this one thing: Silence does not symbolize lack of information or know-how. As a communicator, silence gives an intellectual the space to think. And as a listener, it gives an individual or an audience time to absorb what is being communicated.

The concept of allowing silence will feel very uncomfortable at first, especially if people are watching you in anticipation of a response. Stand firm in your approach and give yourself permission to think.

If you want to let your listener or audience know that you are thinking, you can say one of the following:

- "Give me a moment to gather my thoughts on this."
- "I want to be thoughtful in my response."
- "I'm thinking through the best way to say this."
- "That's a good question. Give me a second."

These responses buy you time and communicate to your listener(s) that you're being reflective and intentional. The ability to slow down to process is especially important in a world that rewards fast replies. We've been conditioned to believe faster is better, but thoughtful always wins.

My best friend is a slow thinker. And I've learned to love that about him. It means he's processing deeply. If you're a slower thinker, you may need to train people around you to expect a slower response. And that's okay.

Volume

The volume at which you speak matters. When someone's excited, their voice naturally rises. That's normal. We also see volume increase in faith-based settings, athletic events, or motivational speeches. But here's where it gets tricky: some speakers use high volume the entire time as a tactic to command attention. And in my experience, it's not always necessary.

I was curious about this, so I did some digging. Turns out, people are more likely to listen to voices that fall within a specific volume and pitch range (Klofstad, Anderson, & Peters, 2012). Pitch plays a big role, too. Higher-pitched voices, often associated with femininity, can be perceived as less authoritative. Lower-pitched voices are often linked with masculinity and command, and retain attention for a longer duration of time.

Think about newscasters, radio personalities, and talk show hosts. Most have deeper voices, not because higher voices are less valid, but because audiences subconsciously associate lower tones with credibility. It's worth considering how your pitch and tone affect how you're received, not to change who you are, but to understand the full scope of how you're heard.

Pace

When people are nervous, they speed up. When people are emotional or upset, they speak faster. That's natural. But the goal of communication is to transfer information. If your words are coming out too quickly, your listener may miss the meaning.

Talking fast can also overwhelm your listener by giving them too much information to process at a time. So, the invitation here is to monitor your speed and breathe. A comfortable pace helps the person on the other side stay with you.

Most people will speak before breathing, run out of air mid-sentence, and end of rushing their words to complete what felt incomplete. To avoid this, think: Inhale. Speak. Breathe. Repeat.

Try This Exercise Belly Breath Activity

1. Inhale through your nose for 4 counts
2. Feel the belly expand
3. Exhale slowly through your mouth for 6 counts
4. On the exhale, say:

"I am learning to speak clearly." Repeat 5 times.

Here's what the research says and how you can measure your speaking pace to own it:

What the Numbers Say

- The average conversational rate in U.S. English is around 150 words per minute (wpm).

- For presentations and TED-style speaking, 140–160 wpm is ideal, consistent with experienced speakers.

- Clear speech, often used in public speaking, ranges from 100–120 wpm.

- Students learning English perform best when spoken to at ~125 wpm.

Why this helps: Speaking too quickly (above 180 wpm) can reduce comprehension; speaking too slowly can feel dull. Aim for a pace that's engaging, understandable, and intentional.

How to Calculate Your Rate of Speech

Step 1: Record Yourself

Use the built-in voice recorder on your phone.

On iPhone

- Open the Voice Memos app

- Tap Record

- Speak naturally at a comfortable pace

- Tap Stop when finished

On Android

- Open the Voice Recorder app

- Tap Record

- Speak clearly and at a steady pace

- Tap Stop

Tip: Place your phone about **12–18 inches** from your mouth and record in a quiet space.

Step 2: Save the Recording

- Give your recording a clear name (*example: Practice Response – Day 1*)

- Save it to your phone

Step 3: Upload the Recording to Google Drive

Open Google Drive

1. Tap the "+" (New) button
2. Select Upload
3. Choose your audio file
4. Wait for the upload to complete

Step 4: Open Google Docs

1. In Google Drive, tap New
2. Select Google Docs
3. Open a blank document

Step 5: Turn On Voice Typing

1. In Google Docs, select Tools
2. Click Voice typing
3. A microphone icon will appear on the screen

Step 6: Play Your Recording

1. Click the microphone icon in Google Docs
2. Play your audio recording out loud
3. Google Docs will transcribe what it hears in real time

Step 7: Do the math

- Talking rate = (word count) ÷ (minutes).
- Example: 155 words in 1 minute = 155 wpm.

Step 8: Compare to the benchmarks

- 100–120 wpm = clear and focused
- 140–160 wpm = confident and engaging

- 160 wpm = fast, great for dynamic energy, but risky for full understanding

You can repeat the exercise across different contexts: fast-paced conversation, measured presentations, and emotional sharing, to understand your range.

Why This Matters

- **Comprehension:** Studies show listeners grasp content better when you speak at a moderate pace (e.g., EFL students performed best at ~125–160 wpm).
- **Trust & Influence:** A controlled pace communicates confidence. Too fast and you may seem anxious; too slow and you may lose credibility.
- **Engagement:** Vary your speed. Slow for emphasis, speed up for excitement while anchoring your baseline in that 140–160 wpm sweet spot.

Tone

Tone is about inflection. It's about how your words sound, not just what you say, but how you say it. A monotone delivery, where every sentence sounds the same, puts people to sleep. Great speakers vary their tone. They emphasize certain words. They soften at the right moments. They use tone to express energy and emotion.

When tone and body language match your message, that's congruent communication. And that's where the magic happens. Your listener hear and feel you, too. Miscommunication happens when your words say one thing, but your tone or body says another.

Here's the main takeaway in all of this: You won't know how you are communicating until you study your visual and vocal identity.

Practice. Record yourself. Watch how your pace, tone, and volume change depending on your environment.

REFLECTION QUESTIONS:

1. How would you describe your current vocal style?
2. Which vocal habits do you want to keep, and which habits would you like to adjust?
3. Do you tend to speak too fast or too softly when nervous?
4. How comfortable are you with silence?
5. How does your tone support or distract from your message?

"...Look, I have put my words in your mouth! Today I appoint you to stand up against nations and kingdoms. Some you must uproot and tear down, destroy and overthrow. Others you must build up and plant." (Jeremiah 1:9-10, NLT)

CHAPTER 10

BUILDING TRUST THROUGH YOUR WORDS

There is the difference between talking and communicating.

Talking is producing a sound from your lips that can be translated into words that are and heard by others. Others can hear the sound; they can process the sound.

Babies and toddlers can talk. Some animals can even "talk" with a few words.

Cashiers talk. Church ushers talk. Cruise staff talk. Movie Theater host talk. Security Officers talk. Talking provides an information transfer.

On the other hand, communicating is an intentional sound that connects the speaker to the lister.

Dog trainers communicate. Therapist communicate. Teachers communicate. Lawyers communicate. Receptionist communicate. Bank tellers communicate.

Communication provides a knowledge transfer. Great communicators are deeply revered for the impact of the words they share with those that they influence.

So, when I'm teaching the skill of verbal competency, I am over emphasizing the importance of what is being said.

Words are not merely information to be shared, they help to formulate HOW the information will be received. When words are intentionally chosen, they bring clarity, emotion, and imagery to the lister.

Let's look at these two sentences:

"For the next 90 days, I want us focused on improving our performance next quarter."

"For the next 90 days, I want us focused on three things: serving customers faster, finishing projects under budget, and celebrating every small win."

Both sentences talk about performance. Only one gives you something you can picture and move toward.

As a leader, your words are not just sentences. Your words are instructions, invitations, affirmations, road maps, and sometimes, healing.

This makes verbal competency an integral part of building your influence.

What Verbal Competency Really Is

When I say, "verbal competency," I'm talking about:

- The words you choose
- The phrases you repeat
- The pictures you paint in people's minds
- The way those words land in someone's body and spirit
- Verbal competency answers questions like:
    - Does what I'm saying make sense to the people listening?
    - Does it sound like me or like I'm pretending to be someone I'm not?
    - Do my words create clarity?
    - Do people feel built up or torn down after I speak?

You already have a verbal style.

The question is: Is it helping you earn your influence?

Simplicity is a Superpower

Some of the most influential leaders I've worked with don't use the fanciest vocabulary. They're not trying to win a spelling bee. They're trying to win hearts, shift culture, and move people toward action. That's why one of the first shifts I ask my students to make is this:

Trade an impressive speech for a speech that can be immediately understood.

Instead of saying:

- "We need to strategically optimize our approach to maximize engagement." Try:
    o "Let's figure out one better way to connect with people this week." Instead of:
- "Per my last email…" Try:
    o "Circling back on this, what do you need from me to move forward?"

The more simplified you can communicate, the clearer you can be, the less resistance people will have to following you.

Make It Visual: Paint Pictures with Your Words

One of the easiest ways to grow your verbal competency is to ask: "Can they see what I'm saying?"

Words like "better," "more," "soon," and "improve" are vague. They don't create a picture.

Now imagine you say:

- "When customers walk into this room, I want it to feel like a warm living room, versus a cold waiting room."

- "When we're done with this project, I want our customers to feel like they've been seen and heard, versus processed and rushed."

See the difference?

The instructions were supported with imagery. You painted a picture so your team can aim their effort at a feeling, not just a task.

Great leaders use:

- **Personal anecdotes** – "When I was in a similar role…"
- **Childhood memories** – "Growing up, my mom always said…"
- **Lessons from past experiences** – "The last time we rushed this, here's what happened…"
- **Analogies and metaphors** – "Think of this like a relay race …"

These little language choices make your message memorable. People may forget your bullet points, but they carry your pictures with them.

Own Your "Leader Language"

Every influential leader I admire has a certain "sound" to them. There are phrases they repeat, values they name, and one-liners that feel like a verbal fingerprint. I call that an individual's Leader Language.

Leader Language is:

- The way you talk about work, calling, and purpose.
- The phrases you lean on when encouraging or correcting someone.
- The sentences people can hear in their head, even when you're not in the room.

For example, my own Leader Language includes things like:

- "What you model, you teach."
- "Every highly skilled person was once mediocre."
- "How you communicate is married to how you feel, the two cannot be divorced."

These phrases that I repeat often come from years of experience, scripture, coaching, and conversations. Over time, they became part of how I lead and communicate.

You have Leader Language inside you, too. Maybe it sounds like:

- "We do hard things in small steps."
- "Done with care is better than done fast."
- "We are in the business of fixing people's problems, faster than we might fix our own."

When you intentionally develop your Leader Language:

- Your team knows what you value.

- Your words become anchors during stressful seasons.

- People begin to act out your leadership values.

And that's influence.

Watch Your Defaults

Let's be honest. Some of our everyday phrases are working against the kind of leader we're working to become.

Listen for default phrases like:

- "It is what it is."

- "That's just how I am."

- "Y'all always mess this up."

- "Nobody ever listens."

Those words carry more weight than you think. As a leader, your words become:

- **Labels** people wear ("I always mess this up.")

- **Limits** people accept ("I'm not leadership material.")

- **Lids** on what your team believes is possible ("We're just a small group; we can't do that.")

Verbal competency means catching those casual, careless phrases and replacing them with **constructive** ones:

Instead of: "We can never get this right."

Try: "This part keeps tripping us up, let's slow it down and walk through it together."

Instead of: "Nobody ever listens."

Try: "I want to make sure we're on the same page. Tell me what you heard so I can clarify anything that's unclear."

Instead of: "That's just how I am."

Try: "I'm still growing in this area, but here's what I'm working on."

These small language adjustments help to change environments and empower the people you lead. These changes also communicate to your team that you are aware of the growth opportunity and are attempting to make strides to improve.

Self-Check Exercise: Audit Your Words

This week, I want you to become a curious observer of your own language.

1. **Record a real moment.**

Audio-record a team huddle, a voice note you send, or a conversation where you're explaining something important.

2. **Play it back.**

Listen like a student, not a critic. What stands out? Are your words:
   * Clear/Confusing
   * Visual/Vague
   * Encouraging/Exhausting

3. **Highlight 3 phrases.**

   * Two phrases you want to keep because they sound like the leader you're becoming.
   * One phrase you want to retire because it doesn't reflect the leader you are anymore.

4. **Rewrite your language.**

Take that one "retired" phrase and write a new, constructive alternative you can use instead.

5. **Practice out loud.**

Say the new phrase in front of a mirror or on a voice note until it feels natural.

REFLECTION QUESTIONS:

1. How would you describe your verbal style today: simple, complicated, direct, soft, encouraging, or blunt?
2. What common phrases do you use that feel like "old you" instead of the leader you're becoming?
3. When has someone's words deeply encouraged you as a leader? What made their language so powerful?
4. Where do you tend to get vague in your communication (expectations, deadlines, feedback)? Why do you think that is?
5. If your team repeated your words when you weren't around, would you be proud of what they're saying?

Additional Exercise

Finish these sentences in your journal or out loud:

- When I speak with clarity, my team feels…
- One phrase I'm retiring as a leader is…
- One phrase I want people to associate with my leadership is…
- When I share stories or examples, I notice that people…

Power Phrases Toolkit:

Use these as practice lines, affirmations, or reminders before you step into a meeting, send a message, or have a hard conversation:

- "My words don't have to be perfect to be powerful."
- "I choose language that builds people, not breaks them."
- "Clarity is kindness. I speak clearly and with care."
- "God can use my everyday words to create extraordinary change."

Verbal competency is about refining the leader you already are so that your words finally match your heart.

SECTION 3: THE START OF YOU

"This is my command—be strong and courageous! Do not be afraid or discouraged. For the LORD your God is with you wherever you go." (Joshua 1:9, NLT)

CHAPTER 11

THE LANGUAGE OF TRUST

During college, I spent my summers working in the Recreation Division of Maryland-National Capital Parks and Planning (M-NCPPC) as a camp counselor. When I started the role, other camp counselors made it very clear that summer was really about one thing-preparing the campers to win the Annual Showcase - basically a talent show hosted in an arena where over 20 camp sites compete for first place.

This was a full production with custom-produced music, choreography, dance stunts, and themed costumes that filled about 35,000 square feet of the Show Place Arena in Upper Marlboro, Maryland. The competition was intense, and every camp wanted to take home that first-place trophy.

The last two summers I worked there, my camp took home the first-place trophy, and I was instrumental in that win. At the time, I was captain of my college step team, so I knew how to choreograph, edit music, plan formations, and lead rehearsals. I brought all those skills to camp, and my campers soaked it all up - practicing and performing their hearts out. We earned a five-foot trophy so big that the only place I could store it was in my mom's basement.

My mom did hair part-time at home, and one of her clients, Coach Yvonne Collins—a high school cheerleading coach—noticed it one day. She asked if I would come work with her cheerleaders at Fairmont Heights High School (FHHS) in Capitol Heights, Maryland. I had never coached cheer before, but I knew performance, preparation, and competition, so I gave it a shot.

At twenty-two years old, I stepped into a gym full of teenage girls, most of them not much younger than me, and some who even looked older. I'll admit, I was intimidated. I didn't know the technical side of cheerleading—stunts, jumps, or injury prevention. I just knew how to put together a performance and grow a competitive team.

For two years, I assisted Coach Collins, helping with choreography and music. Then she accepted a job in Dallas, and just like that, I became the head coach. After two years of going to competitions, severely losing, and watching the cheerleaders not really have the heartbeat of the school spirit, I saw an opportunity to really change the culture of cheer, and also the team's contribution to the athletic department.

When I became head coach, I raised the standard. I implemented new expectations that, at first, the girls did not like. I created a rule that if you didn't have at least a 3.0 GPA, you could stay on the team, but you could not perform. You could wear the uniform, attend practices, and learn the routines, but you would not get "on the line."

I also introduced a character rule. If anyone on the team received a disciplinary report from a teacher or administrator, the entire team would crab the track—bent knees, frog walk, all the way around, rain or shine. I wanted them to understand that membership on the team represented more than athletic ability. It represented leadership, and more importantly, it represented me.

I even outlawed yelling. We could be firm, but not loud and demeaning to each other. I told them, "I'm not going to speak to you in a disrespectful way because I don't want you speaking to me that way." Some of the girls didn't know how to process that. They were used to being yelled at to be motivated. For them, leadership and aggression were the same thing. Not only was that not my temperament, but I also wanted to show them a different way of leadership.

We started fundraising to pay for tumbling and stunt camps, hosting car washes and bake sales, even performing on street corners with donation buckets. We raised enough funds to upgrade uniforms (this hadn't been done in over 5 years) and attend cheer training camp. I pushed them **hard**, but I loved them hard, too.

That first year as head coach, we didn't place at the competition, but the girls were strong, their endurance was up, and they had grown tremendously. The next year, we placed third (for the first time in the school's history), and that changed everything. Tryouts the following season were jammed packed. Girls wanted to be part of the program. The same team that once resisted my standards now carried pride in meeting them.

My four years as a high school cheerleading coach taught me that people rise to the expectations you hold of them- even if they initially resist at first.

There was one skill in particular that I actively applied to grow the unity of my team. When I applied this one skill, I noticed that my girls' confidence grew, and so did their courage to be placed in new positions and to lead team tasks. That skill was providing feedback in the language of praise.

The Power of Praise

There are two main types of praise: private and public.

The first type of praise is private praise. This approach is intimate. It's one-on-one acknowledgment that says, I see you. This type of praise is deliberately intentional, considering that the person delivering the praise would have to initiate a form of alone time or carve out time to seek out a person to talk. This form of communication fosters trust between the communicator and the recipient. Some people — especially those who are more introverted or uncomfortable with the spotlight—need and/or prefer this kind of connection.

As a holistic public speaking coach today, I still apply this approach with adults that I coach and train. During our one-on-one sessions, I verbally highlight their effort and contributions. I praise them for their decision-making and their decisiveness. When I listen in to their thought process and how they arrive at conclusions, I may even praise the boundaries they uphold or societal pressures they choose not to feed. Any opportunity I get when listening, I'm listening for little and big wins to highlight that are easy to run right past. No matter how small or big the praise/acknowledgment is, some individuals struggle to receive the praise.

They say things like, "yeah, but I still need to" or "Now if I can only." Depending on a person's view of their self- concept, praise may be hard to receive because they simply don't feel that they have arrived at their measure of success. To these individuals, there remains a gap between who they are and where they would like to be. In this case, for them, praise is not only hard to receive, but it's also something they do not believe about themselves.

The next time you try private praise, watch carefully the body language of the person you are praising. Do they maintain eye contact? Do they scratch their head or shake their head in disagreement? If they struggle to believe what you shared, spend a little extra time affirming what you share.

Ways to Affirm Your Praise

1. Give a recent example of the person's contribution and its impact.
2. Share how the impact positively affected your organization.
3. Share how the impact affects you as their leader.

Sometimes we have to give data to individuals who don't see the results of their work. If you take the time to praise, please also take the time to ensure individuals understand why you are acknowledging them.

In Front of Others

The second type of praise is public praise. This type of praise happens in front of others. Others can be team members or adjacent team members, stakeholders, etc. This can be done at a meeting, in a pre-event huddle, closing out a call, or from the stage at the opening of an event. It is commonly perceived that the larger the group and the more influential the viewers, the more significant the praise means. Think of galas, board meetings, award shows, etc. These are examples of social settings where public praise is demonstrated. Where recipients are publicly affirmed and recognized.

Public praise signals what you, as the leader, value and want to see repeated. Think closely about that. When you recognize a behavior or attribute publicly, you are communicating that behavior or attribute is something you want to see more of. So, when you publicly recognize someone, you're not just affirming them; you're communicating the standard for the entire group.

You're communicating:

- This is what we celebrate here.
- This is what we want to see more of.
- This is the kind of behavior/attributes we value and support.
- This is what we envisioned when we created this organization.

My rule of thumb is to **always praise someone publicly for the praise already given to them privately.** Without that personal connection point, public praise can feel less meaningful (sort of like declaring your love for someone in front of an audience but never professing your love to that person in private). As you're working to build genuine trust within a team, your continuity of communication is a great foundation for trust. What you share in private should mirror what you bring up publicly, allowing there to be no doubt of sincerity or truthfulness.

Lastly, if the individuals are anything like a former colleague of mine, Elizabeth, public praise could make them feel completely uncomfortable. It may be challenging for them to bask in the recognition while also fighting feelings of embarrassment or anxiety. The public recognition for these individuals is not an esteem builder;

it repels their interest and connection. It's good to know your person or people before engaging in public feedback.

When people trust that your praise is meaningful and genuine, it will open doors of vulnerability that allow them to receive correction and other feedback from you.

I tell leaders all the time: **if you struggle to express appreciation or affirm others, you'll struggle to build trust. Every healthy relationship, personal or professional, requires emotional reciprocity.** Without it, the connection is temporary, strained, and frail.

REFLECTION & APPLICATION:

1. When was the last time I intentionally praised someone on my team or in my circle?
2. Was it public, private, or both?
3. How did they respond?
4. Which form of praise feels most natural for me to give, public or private, and which one do I avoid? Why?
5. Do I give acknowledgment only when performance is exceptional, or do I also celebrate effort and growth?
6. What message am I communicating through the things I choose to praise publicly?

The Conflict That Taught Me to Listen

Every team has that one person who stretches your patience and teaches you what leadership really requires of you. They passionately disrupt your way of thinking, and in some cases, they challenge your processes and authority. It can feel like they don't agree with your planning and struggle to respect your authority. You sometimes might want to ask them, "Do you want MY job?"

Have you experienced this? Well, I have. In every leadership role, I've found these individuals to be a thorn and also a mirror- uncovering my insecurities and strengthening my conflict muscle.

Shanice wasn't my first encounter with this, but she is the encounter that I vividly remember. Shanice was an upperclassman on my varsity cheerleading team at FHHS. She was the kind of athlete who proudly and unapologetically knew her talent. She had a confidence about her that never dimmed, even when it came to her academics. Her teachers describe her as smart and opinionated. She shared ideas freely and often communicated her observations. She brought those exact character traits to my team. Along with her personality, athletically she was an amazing jumper, strong base for stunts, and had a powerhouse voice- basically the full package.

During one practice, Shanice made a comment that cut deep. I can't remember her exact words, but it was something close to, "It's not like you know what you're doing anyway." She was referring to my feedback on our competition routine that we were building. Her comment probably came out of frustration because of the changes being made to formations and sequences.

After her comment, the room went silent as her words rang in my head. I had always felt slightly insecure about my lack of cheerleading experience when I traveled to other schools and saw the other coaches. Their language and skill sets were apparent, as many of them had been in their role for over 10 years. And me, well, I was learning as I went, teaching myself the sport and occasionally investing in cheer coach clinics. While I was confident about the character of the team I was building, I also carried the pressure of proving to my team that I was skilled enough to coach them. So, Shanice's words triggered that inner child in me—the version of myself that feared not being good enough.

I didn't respond to Shanice. I called for a break and allowed the girls to catch their breath. Or rather, for myself to process what had happened. I remembered being angry and embarrassed. Eventually, practice resumed, and I dismissed the girls at our normal end time. Still never acknowledging the comment.

Over the next few practices, Shanice made more small comments. Like things under her breath. Things that didn't sting as badly, but it was obvious that she was poking at my patience. I guess my silence gave her words permission to continue. Then the subtle comments grew into blatant disrespect. Weeks later, after another public remark, I finally called her mother and asked if she was available for a meeting. I spent the day prior writing down all the occurrences, their times, and the inappropriate statements Shanice said.

Her mom was very receptive and came to meet with me the very next day. When the three of us sat down, I explained to Shanice's mom what had been happening. She listened intently. It was clear to me that the behavior I was explaining was not a behavior Shanice's mom tolerated. She assured me that she would talk with Shanice and that this would not be an issue going forward. Before we wrapped up our conversation, her mom asked me something that really had me thinking, "Why didn't you tell me the first time the behavior happened?"

I didn't have an answer that I was proud to say, so I didn't say anything. I shrugged. The truth was, I feared engaging in conflict with Shanice. Would things escalate? Would I lose my composure if she said something further provoking? Would she respect my authority if I spoke up? The unknown was too risky.

Avoidance is agreement in disguise. Shanice taught me that.

Running to Conflict to Protect Harmony

After the meeting with Shanice and her mom, the next day, I sat down with Shanice one-on-one. I told her, "I want to apologize if the expectations I've set sometimes make you feel like I'm pushing you too hard. That's never my intent. I want the best for you and our team."

<table>
<tr><td>SOMETHING TO THINK ABOUT</td></tr>
<tr><td>Do you have someone on your team who triggers an insecurity in you? Have you given some thought as to why?</td></tr>
</table>

She looked at me and said, "Coach, I'm sorry for what I said. You're a great coach. I know you're learning, but you're really doing a great job."

My eyes filled immediately hearing her validation, but I held back the tears.

Even though I was in a position of authority, I still had feelings of inadequacy, questioning my decisions and judgment. If I was being too hard on the team or not hard enough. Shanice's words were comforting, and they felt sincere.

I realized then that I had never taken the time to affirm or praise Shanice or talk with her one-on-one. In fact, I subconsciously didn't feel it was necessary. In my mind, she didn't need more validation or connection, and her confidence repelled my interest in further affirming her. Actually, her confidence and advanced skill triggered a lack of confidence in me.

Conflict is Complex

The conversation with Shanice might have lasted 5 minutes, but internally, it left a lasting feeling of relief in my body, kind of like the relief you get when you work through your first conflict as a new couple with someone you're dating: Going into the conversation, you are aware of the impact the exchange can have on the relationship, but you decide to move forward with it because the issue matters to you and the lack of communication is affecting you. That's what happened with the encounter with Shanice. As my body was releasing the tension of unspoken feelings and expectations, our relationship was being repaired. At the same time, a "conflict muscle" was forming in my body, and the fear of having hard conversations was beginning to leave my body.

When I train organizations today, I remind them that conflict is human and unavoidable. In addition to being unavoidable, conflict reveals your vulnerability as you convey the source of your ideas, thoughts, and expectations. Think about that. When you are having a conflict with someone, it is because your expectation of their behavior is not being met. In healthy conflict, in order to address the behavior, you have to acknowledge the unmet expectation.

Out of all the skills I teach, conflict is one that never leaves a dry eye in the room. Many people feel unequipped to address the "hard stuff" in their professional and personal relationships. They fear judgment, rejection, and even the possibility of an unfavorable response.

In my keynote, *Having Hard Conversations Softly*, I ask the room to raise their hand if they have an overdue hard conversation that they are avoiding. Every time, every hand goes up. Sometimes, the hands go up before I even finish my statement. Unspoken conflict is robbing teams of improved performance and synergy, and it robs relationships of compounded connection.

While I've read many books on conflict, I've never seen anyone break down resolving conflict holistically- considering your whole self, your understanding, and your support.

The TALK Method is something that I developed to teach addressing conflict in your personal or professional life. If you'd like to learn more about applying the TALK Method to your team, reach out to schedule a consultation.

The TALK Method

T: Take Assessment

Start by assessing yourself. Conflict is evidence that your values (or the established organization's values) are being challenged. Take my situation: Excellence is one of my core values, so Shanice's comment about my coaching ability felt like a threat to me performing my duties as a coach with the highest quality of effort. Instinctively, I wanted to defend or stand up for a character trait that I proudly work to honor.

What do you value? Do you value time, effort, efficiency, usefulness, etc.? When any of these areas are challenged or ignored, or even discarded, how do you instinctively respond? With this information, before addressing a conflict with someone else, pause and ask yourself, why did that really bother me? What am I feeling? What am I protecting?

A: Ask Questions

Once you've taken the assessment, go to the other person with curiosity, not accusation. Ask, "Can we talk about what happened?" or "When you said X, can you help me understand what you meant?"

The goal is to curiously understand the motive, feelings, and meaning behind a behavior. You may not agree with what they share, and you don't have to; however, can you work to accept (love) them enough to respect what they share?

The second greatest commandment is to "…love your neighbor as yourself. There is no commandment greater than these." (Mark 12:31, NIV)

Our neighbor isn't always a close relative or friend, sometimes it's the person in the drive-thru, or the teller at the bank. Love for God (and for others) will gift you a capacity to genuinely be curious about people and willingly allow you to ask questions.

Here are some examples of questions to ask others to help you explore your curiosity about them:

- What really ticks you off?
- What causes immediate conflict for you?
- What do you need more of from me?
- What is your vision for the project?
- What does success look like for you?
- What does commitment look like for you?
- How can I show more engagement?
- What blind spots do you see that I may be missing?
- How can we make things better?
- What behaviors have you observed from me that may hinder our success?

- What type of learning opportunities should we pursue as a team?

- What is our "WIN" for this project/opportunity?

When you receive answers to these questions, consider the responses as sacred emotional data points. For private people, this is a very sacred space. For people who might not be so private, this is still a level of access that they are willingly granting you. Handle this privilege with care.

L: Listen to Understand

Listening is just as hard as public speaking. It requires energy, emotional regulation, and effort. Energy is required to listen because a great listener will be experiencing the emotions or assimilating them in their mind while processing what is being shared. A great listener visualizes things and also puts themselves in the shoes of the person speaking. A *great* listener follows along to get context and to affirm the experience of the person speaking. If you don't think that's energy, just try listening to someone who is deeply disappointed by something, and you are sleep deprived. Not only will you miss some of the things they are saying, but you will also struggle with empathizing with how they feel.

Listening also requires emotional regulation. You may hear things you deeply disagree with or things that evoke anger or confusion in your mind. Something could be said that is not true or overlooks other factors (and you know this).

A *great* listener applies restraint from speaking about the very thing they feel triggered by so that they are not a distraction from what the person is trying to communicate. In plain terms, emotional

> **What is emotion?**
>
> Emotion is a conscious first displayed in the body. For example, anxiety can show up as shortness of breath, perspiration. Excitement can show up as jittery movement in the body. Anger can show up as increased body heat and heart pulsations. Why does this matter to you? Emotions affect the body by releasing secretions like dopamine or cortisol, and the release of secretions affects how we speak and feel.

regulation is recognizing an emotion in the body, naming it, and choosing not to allow the emotion to become a feeling. So, when we talk about emotional regulation, we are choosing to manage a bodily reaction before it becomes an outward response in how we communicate. In conflict, emotional regulation is a true cheat code to having healthy

conflict (which ultimately builds the resilience of any relationship).

K: Know When to Ask for Help

Some conflicts just won't have an easy resolution. Perhaps both parties are not able to take assessment, ask questions, and listen. Each of those steps requires a level of emotional maturing that not all are ready to practice. Or in some cases, they may not have the skills to do so. Even if you, as the initiator, may be able to do all the above, healthy conflict still requires two willing people.

The truth is, not everyone is ready, willing, or capable. In these cases, you will have to ask for help. This looks like bringing in someone neutral to help facilitate a conversation about the conflict.

"If your brother sins against you, go and tell him his fault, between you and him alone. If he listens to you, you have gained your brother. But if he does not listen, take one or two others along with you." (Matthew 18:15–16, ESV)

The goal is not to win the disagreement but to protect the relationship.

The Language of Trust

Conflict handled well can become a doorway to a deeper connection. Every hard conversation is an opportunity to strengthen understanding and increase your ability to practically influence someone.

1. When conflict arises, what is my default response: avoidance, defensiveness, or curiosity?

2. How quickly do I address tension within my team, and what story do I tell myself when I delay it?

3. In what ways have I been afraid of having hard conversations, and how has that fear affected the trust within my relationships or team?

4. Which part of the TALK method do I need to strengthen—taking assessment, asking questions, listening to understand, or knowing when to ask for help?

5. How can I create a culture around me, whether at work, home, or in ministry, where open dialogue and acknowledgment are the norm?

"Do not turn away from her (Wisdom) and she will guard and protect you; Love her, and she will watch over you." (Proverbs 4:6, AMP)

CHAPTER 12

TRUST EROSION

We often think trust is broken only in big, critical moments, like when something said in confidence is shared publicly, or when a promise is made and never fulfilled. Those are trust breaches, and they sting deeply. But in leadership, trust is not always eroded in one moment. More often, it shows up in small, consistent ways.

It happens when we overpromise and underdeliver. When we commit to a meeting and show up late. When we forget to send the materials, we said we would. When we tell a team member, we'll advocate for them and then get too busy to follow through. These small breaks, left unaddressed, slowly erode credibility.

And without trust, there is no influence.

Here are some subtle, less obvious ways we as leaders breed mistrust—ways that seem small in the moment but create big cracks over time.

1. Setting Standards We Don't Model

One of the fastest ways to break trust with your team is to set a standard that you yourself cannot meet.

If you expect your team to always have a positive attitude, do you bring that same energy when you walk into a meeting after a stressful day? If your standard is direct communication, do you address issues with honesty, or do you avoid them and hope they fix themselves? If you tell people to prioritize their family, do you model that in your family by honoring family commitments that come at the expense of disappointing others?

Your behavior needs to consistently match your message.

2. Living in Fragments

Another way trust weakens is through fragmentation. This happens when we show up as different versions of ourselves depending on where we are.

We have a "work version" of ourselves, a "family version," and a "social version." Each one adapts to its environment, and while that may seem like flexibility, what it often creates is disconnection.

When you live fragmented, your development becomes fragmented too.

Instead of compounding your growth—building on the same principles and core values across all areas of life, you start over in each environment. Every version of you needs development. Every version of you needs healing. Every version of you needs to learn communication, conflict resolution, and self-advocacy.

When you choose to be one version of yourself everywhere, your growth is continuous, it compounds and matures.

Let the calm, self-aware version of you that leads meetings also lead your family. Let the thoughtful version of you that encourages your friends also engage your coworkers. Let the compassionate version of you that prays for others also show up for the people who challenge you.

When you do this, there's no confusion about who you are.

When there is a disconnect between who you are at work and who you are at home, that is your yellow flag signaling misalignment. Whenever you are misaligned, you are more likely to experience exhaustion and carry a weight you are not designed to carry.

"For my yoke *is* easy and my burden is light." (Matthew 11:30, NKJV)

What you are designed to carry, you will be graced for (giving you provision to carry out your role with divine power, strength, wisdom, etc.).

3. Sometimey Integrity

Integrity is not location-based. It's not something we put on like a blazer before a meeting and take off once we get home. Integrity is consistent alignment of your actions, character, and words across every environment.

Some people believe that what happens outside of work doesn't matter as long as you're effective inside the workplace. I disagree. The person you are when no one is watching is the same person that people will eventually meet when pressure is high.

If you lack integrity in your personal life, it will show up in your professional relationships. If you're inconsistent in your commitments outside of work, it will eventually bleed into your leadership style.

When you are the same person in every space - honest and accountable, it builds a deep sense of safety for those who follow you. They know what to expect from you. There's no guessing which version of you will show up today.

That kind of consistency creates psychological safety. It builds loyalty. And it invites others to bring their whole selves to the table too.

REFLECTION & APPLICATION:

1. What expectations do I hold my team accountable to that I may not consistently meet myself?

2. Do I set standards that even I struggle to maintain? How can I better model what I ask of others?

3. Where in my life am I living in fragments—showing up as one person in one space and another somewhere else?

4. What does alignment look like for me right now?

    - Am I the same person at work, at home, and in my social life?

    - Where do I feel the biggest gap?

5. How does inconsistency in my character affect how people experience my leadership?

6. How can I start practicing continuity between who I say I am and how I show up?

"If people are proud, they will soon become ashamed. But if people are humble, they become wise." (Proverbs 11:2, EASY)

CHAPTER 13

INFLUENCE VS AUTHORITY

Why Do You Want to Lead?

I wish I could ask every leader I meet this exact question. Not because it sounds good or makes for a great icebreaker, but because it forces a pause. It gets to the real root of why so many teams struggle under poor leadership. I don't think most people actually want to lead. People want the benefits of leadership: the title, the salary, the access, the visibility. But leadership itself? The daily weight of it? That's a different story.

Leadership is an ongoing, ever-evolving responsibility that centers around people. Yes, people those unpredictable, emotional, talented, complex humans you become accountable to and held accountable for. They're not just relying on your task management or your ability to hit deadlines, they're depending on your consistency, your fairness, your emotional steadiness, and your guidance. They're watching how you respond to pressure, how you treat others when things don't go as planned, and how you lead through uncertainty. That's what leadership really is: the daily, human-centered effort to lead people with care and integrity.

In leadership, you eat the mistakes of others. You clean up messes you didn't create. Your tasks don't have a finish line. You're expected to build capacity, carry the team through rough patches, and keep morale high, even when you're exhausted. Depending on what you're leading, there might be financial targets to hit, key performance indicators (KPIs) to measure, and deliverables to present.

Leadership is hard.

So, let me ask again: why would you sign up for this?

I believe most leaders fall into one of three core identity groups when it comes to their leadership motivations: those in pursuit of a lifestyle, those seeking the spotlight, and those who crave control.

Lifestyle Seekers are drawn to leadership because of the lifestyle upgrades it can offer. They're not just daydreaming about a promotion; they're envisioning a better car, luxurious travel, early retirement, or being able to swipe their card without consideration of their budget or available resources. For these leaders, the role is a bridge to financial ease, personal freedom, and experiences that are currently just out of reach. Leadership, to them, is the route to design the life they've always envisioned, and they're willing to take on more if it brings that vision closer to reality.

Front Page Lovers crave visibility and recognition. They light up when their name is associated with excellence, when they are the voice quoted in the room, or when their picture lands on the announcements. They aren't just in it for the win, they want people to know they contributed to it. It's not enough to do good work. They feel most fulfilled when their contribution is acknowledged, spotlighted, and celebrated.

Driver's Seat Addicts thrive on control and execution. These are the folks who aren't necessarily seeking applause or lifestyle upgrades. They just want to be in the driver's seat because they genuinely believe they can steer the ship more efficiently. They trust their instincts, know their strengths, and believe in their systems. Their joy is in the doing, in the progress, and in the results. They love a checklist, live for milestones, and get a rush from watching a vision unfold step by step. For them, crossing the finish line is intrinsically satisfying. They're usually the builders (sometimes even the fixers) who enjoy behind-the-scenes work more than standing on stage taking credit.

Again, none of these motivators are inherently wrong. In fact, recognizing which one resonates most with you can offer deeper clarity on how you lead and what fuels your decisions.

Lifestyle Seekers are motivated by the material rewards that come with leadership. More responsibility typically means more money. These are the people who evaluate opportunities by asking: Does this promotion raise my income? Can I finally get that house or car I've had on my vision board for years? Will I be able to afford better vacations, support my child's education, or just breathe easier when the bills are due? For them, leadership is a strategic pathway to personal freedom and financial peace.

Front Page Lovers are in it for the recognition. They enjoy being acknowledged, celebrated, and seen. They like to own a project, lead a charge, and get credit for what they've built. They are fueled by the spotlight. It's not necessarily about being flashy or self-absorbed. For them, the recognition affirms their hard work and creativity. They want to feel seen for the excellence they bring. They light up when their name is associated with success, and they often use that visibility as fuel to continue growing and performing. It motivates them, encourages them, and keeps them going even in tough seasons.

Driver's Seat Addicts are your high-control achievers. They don't always care for the spotlight, but they do care about getting things done right. They think, "If I lead it, I know it'll get done properly." These leaders are obsessed with execution and thrive on structure, systems, and self-sufficiency. They're known for stepping in when others hesitate, taking full ownership of outcomes, and bringing a laser-sharp focus to every goal. Their validation doesn't come from applause, it comes from results. They feel most energized when they are crossing tasks off a list, hitting stretch goals, and moving projects from vision to reality. For them, leadership is about effectiveness, efficiency, and follow-through.

So, pause for a moment and ask yourself: Why are you in your current leadership role? And if you are pursuing a leadership role, why now?

Why do you want to lead? Be honest. Your answer matters.

Understanding your "why" is essential, because it will help you determine when to lead with authority and when to lead with influence.

Authority

Authority is a pre-established relationship. It's when your professional title signals that you are in charge. In a traditional hierarchy, this means people tend to treat you with a default level of respect based on your role, not necessarily because they know or trust you. Your title acts as your access card. People may address you with formality, approach with caution, or even feel hesitant to be fully themselves in your presence.

Authoritative leaders tend to focus on presentation and perception. They ask themselves, "Do I look confident enough? Do I sound like a leader? Their approach often leans top-down, which can unintentionally create emotional distance and limit connection.

Here are signs you may be operating with an authority-first leadership style:

1. Your team avoids making decisions when you're not around.
2. You are the only voice opening and closing meetings.
3. You lack personal connection with most team members.
4. You struggle with culture-building and people development.
5. You see "team bonding" as a distraction rather than an asset.
6. People go quiet when you enter the room, or say you're hard to approach.
7. You've been told that team members do not feel safe sharing problems with you.

Authority isn't always negative. There are moments when you have to use it to set boundaries, make urgent decisions, or protect people from harm. But when your identity as a leader is built only on authority, you end up leading distantly, not relationally.

Now contrast this with the power of earned influence.

Influence

Leaders who lead with influence are deeply connected to their people by fostering real relationships. They know their teammates, not just by name, but by story. They remember anniversaries, ask about kids and pets, and check in when someone seems off. They study what lights their team up and create space for those passions to be seen and respected.

They make time for check-ins that aren't just about tasks but about the person. They celebrate milestones big and small, and when they ask, "How are you doing?" it's genuine. They understand the meaning of people feeling seen, supported, and safe. And when challenges arise, these leaders already have a trust bank built with those they lead.

Here are signs that you lead with influence:

1. You make a conscious effort to remember names.
2. You build relationships before you assign tasks.
3. You ask how someone is doing before pointing out a performance issue.
4. People feel at ease sharing vulnerable things with you (unrelated to work).
5. You invest in learning the strengths and interests of those you lead.

6. You tend to keep relationships long after your time in an organization has ended.
7. You have a history of building up others to take on leadership roles.

These leaders are often the ones called in to de-escalate situations, resolve conflicts, and handle the tough stuff because they're the most trusted.

There are moments when you'll need to lead with authority. But if I had to choose one approach to lead with for the rest of my life, it would be **influence, every single time. Because influence leaves behind a legacy of connection. It creates relationships that outlast the role.**

The Legacy of Influence

My good friend Darryl Bellamy Jr. is someone who influenced me long before we ever became friends. We were introduced by a mutual friend, Greg E. Hill. I remember how generous Darryl was with his knowledge. He gave me so many gems about the speaking business, real gems. He even introduced me to my first professional speaking agency.

To this day, Darryl remains someone who shows up, encourages, and pours into me. So, when he gives feedback, calls me out, or challenges my thinking (which he does often), I listen. I want to listen. I trust him.

Same with Mr. Jones, my first mentor. I met him in eighth grade while navigating peer pressure and learning how to stand up for myself. Mr. Jones has been in my corner ever since. He's cheered for me across decades. When he offers advice, I receive it wholeheartedly. His influence has stood the test of time because he genuinely cares.

This is what influence does. It gives you access, not just to people's behavior, but to their hearts. It earns you a seat in the most sacred places: their mind and their ears.

Influence helps you resolve conflict faster. It breaks team silos. It builds a culture of connection. It develops and multiplies strong future leaders.

So, if someone ever asks you, "As a leader, do you want authority or do you want influence?" I hope your answer sounds something like this:

"I want sustainable connection with those I lead… and that can only be done with influence."

REFLECTION QUESTIONS:

1. What originally drew you to leadership?

2. Are you a Lifestyle Seeker, Front Page Lover, or Driver's Seat Addict? How does that affect your leadership style?

3. In what areas of your leadership do you rely on authority? Where do you lead with influence?

4. Who influenced you in your life? What about their leadership made you trust them?

5. How can you intentionally lead with more influence in your current role?

"Work willingly at whatever you do, as though you were working for the Lord rather than for people." (Colossians 3:23, NLT)

CHAPTER 14

EARN YOUR INFLUENCE

Influence is about what your team believes about your heart. Do they believe you're for them? Do they feel safe bringing you the hard things? Do they trust that you care more about their growth than your image?

That's not something you can demand. That's something you have to earn.

Earning your influence is not a one-time achievement. It's a lifestyle. Most of your influence is earned when nobody's clapping and nobody's posting about it.

- Influence is built when you return the phone call you said you would.
- Influence is built when you apologize without adding excuses.
- Influence is built when you keep someone's secret instead of turning their vulnerability into casual conversation.
- Influence is built when you show up prepared because you value people's time.

Those moments don't seem glamorous. No one is handing you an award for following through on a Tuesday email. But every time you do what you said you would do, you make a small deposit into someone's trust account.

Think of your influence like a bank.

Every act of integrity, consistency, and care is a deposit. Every broken promise, dismissive comment, or careless action is a withdrawal.

You cannot withdraw what you have not been consistently depositing.

When a crisis hits, when you have to make a tough call, when you need to ask more of your team than usual that's when the balance in that trust account really shows. If you've been making deposits over time, people will lean in, even if they don't love the decision, because they trust your heart. If you haven't, you may technically "win" the moment with authority, but you'll lose something deeper in the process.

Earning your influence means deciding that the small, quiet choices matter just as much as the big, public ones.

Consistency Over Charisma

We live in a world that celebrates charisma. The loudest voice, the flashiest presentation, the most confident personality, those are often the people we're told are "natural leaders."

Charisma says, "Look at me."

Consistency says, "You can count on me."

People might initially be drawn to you because of your gifting your speaking, your strategy, your creativity, your ability to get things done. But they stay because of your patterns.

You earn influence by being the same person on and off the stage. By showing up with the same values in meetings, group chats, one-on- ones, and family dinners. By letting people see that the version of you they admire publicly is the same version they encounter privately.

Influence is not about impressing people once. It's about impacting them repeatedly.

Serving Before Shining

One of my favorite things about Jesus's leadership is that He never had to fight for a title. He didn't spend His time arguing about where His name appeared on the flyer. He didn't demand special treatment. He washed feet. He sat with people others avoided. He served.

If anyone deserved authority, it was Him.

And yet, He modeled influence through service.

Earning your influence means being more interested in who people become under your leadership than how impressive you look while leading them.

It means asking questions like:

- Who am I becoming while I lead?

- What is it like to be led by me?

- Do people feel closer to their purpose, their potential, and, yes, even to God, because they are in my orbit?

Your leadership is not just about the goals you hit. It's about the people you form. It means you're not shining alone. You're bringing people with you.

That is the heart of earned influence: not building a platform that only holds you, but building a foundation that can hold many.

Living as an Influential Leader

As you grow in your leadership, I want you to remember this:

Influence is not a gift some people are born with, and others are not. Influence is a series of decisions you make over and over again.

- Decisions to tell the truth.

- Decisions to keep your word.

- Decisions to listen longer than feels comfortable.

- Decisions to slow down and really see people.

- Decisions to say "I don't know, but I'll find out" instead of pretending.

You won't get it right every day. No leader does. But if you commit to earning your influence by showing up with integrity, intention, and care, people will feel it over time.

They may not always agree with every choice you make. They may challenge you. They may have seasons where they struggle with your decisions. But they will know this: you are a leader who takes seriously the responsibility of being trusted.

And that matters.

REFLECTION QUESTIONS:

1. What are three small, consistent actions you can start taking this week to make deposits into your "trust account" with the people you lead?
2. Think of a time when a leader lost some of your trust. What specifically happened, and what could they have done to repair it?
3. In what ways has charisma (yours or someone else's) overshadowed the need for consistency? How do you want to shift that going forward?

4. If the people you lead described your leadership in one sentence, what do you hope they would say? What needs to change for that to be true?

Additional Exercise

Finish these sentences in your journal or out loud:

- People can count on me to…

- One relationship where I want to rebuild trust is…

- When I lead with service instead of ego, I notice that…

You may never know all the ways your influence is shaping lives. But I promise you this: when you choose to earn it day by day, conversation by conversation, God can take your ordinary faithfulness and turn it into a legacy far bigger than anything you could have forced with authority alone.

"So, as God's own chosen people, who are holy [set apart, sanctified for His purpose] and well-beloved [by God himself], **put on a heart of compassion, kindness, humility, gentleness, and patience [which has the power to endure whatever injustice or unpleasantness comes with good temper]** bearing graciously with one another, and willingly forgiving each other if one has a cause for complaint against another; just as the Lord has forgiven you, so should you forgive." (Colossians 3:12-13, AMP)

NOTES

These notes provide context, research references, and additional insight that support concepts explored throughout Earn Your Influence. Scripture references are cited within the text and drawn from the versions noted.

Chapter 1: Foundations of Influence

1. The distinction between authority and influence is widely explored in leadership literature emphasizing trust, credibility, and relational leadership rather than positional power.
2. The account of David and Goliath is found in 1 Samuel 17, illustrating preparation in obscurity as a leadership principle.
3. The concept that people follow leaders whose behavior aligns with their words is supported by research on behavioral integrity in leadership (Simons, 2002).

Chapter 2: The Work That Shapes You

1. Competency and capacity development are core principles in adult learning theory and professional growth models emphasizing deliberate practice and reflective experience.
2. Faithfulness in small responsibilities as preparation for greater responsibility is a recurring biblical leadership theme (Luke 16:10).

Chapter 3: Finding a Voice You Trust

1. Exposure therapy principles show that repeated engagement with feared activities (such as public speaking) reduces anxiety over time.
2. Confidence development is linked to mastery experiences, one of the strongest predictors of self-efficacy (Bandura, 1997).

Chapter 4: When Decisions Compound

1. Identity-based habit formation suggests small decisions create long-term behavioral change (Clear, 2018).
2. Language adaptation across environments is commonly studied in sociolinguistics as code-switching and communicative flexibility.

Chapter 5: Owning Your Evolution

1. Early communication modeling aligns with attachment theory and social learning theory, which show that interpersonal patterns are learned through observation and reinforcement.
2. Emotional regulation practices such as journaling and reflective questioning are evidence-based strategies in cognitive behavioral therapy.

Chapter 6: You Can't Perfect Who You Pretend to Be

1. Authentic leadership research highlights alignment between identity, values, and behavior as a predictor of trust and well-being (Walumbwa et al., 2008).
2. Adaptation for acceptance is often explored in trauma-informed coaching and identity performance research.

Chapter 7: The Cost of Owning Your Faith

1. Identity integration — aligning personal belief with professional expression — is associated with increased meaning and resilience in work (Duffy et al., 2018).
2. The Great Commission appears in Matthew 28:19–20.

Chapter 8: What People Experience When They See You

1. Willis & Todorov (2006) found that people form trustworthiness judgments within approximately 100 milliseconds of seeing a face.
2. Nonverbal communication research consistently shows body language influences perceived credibility and confidence.

Chapter 9: Building Trust Through Your Voice

1. Average conversational speaking rate in English ranges around 150 words per minute; slower rates improve comprehension for complex material.

2. Klofstad, Anderson, & Peters (2012) found vocal pitch influences perceptions of leadership and competence.

Chapter 10: Building Trust Through Your Words

1. Clear communication improves team performance, reduces ambiguity, and strengthens psychological safety (Edmondson, 1999).
2. Narrative and metaphor increase message retention and emotional engagement.

Chapter 11: The Language of Trust

1. Praise as a feedback mechanism is linked to motivation theory and reinforcement learning.
2. Psychological safety increases when leaders balance affirmation with constructive feedback (Google Project Aristotle).

Chapter 12: Trust Erosion

1. Trust erosion often occurs through repeated small inconsistencies rather than singular failures (Covey, Speed of Trust).
2. Behavioral modeling is one of the strongest predictors of culture adoption.

Chapter 13: Influence vs. Authority

1. Relational leadership research shows influence creates longer-lasting commitment than compliance-based authority.
2. Leadership motivation categories reflect intrinsic and extrinsic motivation frameworks (Self-Determination Theory).

Chapter 14: Earn Your Influence

1. Consistency is a primary driver of credibility and trust formation across leadership studies.
2. Servant leadership principles emphasize service, humility, and people development as pathways to influence (Greenleaf, 1970).

INDEX

Bring the Book to Life

In 2026, purchase 50 or more copies of Earn Your Influence and Linnita will waive her speaking fee to facilitate a live Fireside Chat for your group.

Beginning in 2027, the minimum increases to 200 copies. Travel fees are excluded. Visit linnitahosten.com to learn more.